STAY SAFE AT WORK

Your Ultimate
Guide to
Workplace Security

by Steve Albrecht & Robert May

Stay Safe at Work
Your Ultimate Guide to Workplace Security
Second Edition
Copyright © 2021 - 2023 Steve Albrecht

Mainstream Unlimited
800-831-5529

Dr. Robert May Biem47@outlook.com
www.MainstreamUnlimited.com

Publishing Coordinator – Sharon Kizziah-Holmes

Paperback-Press
an imprint of A & S Publishing
Paperback Press, LLC
Springfield, Missouri

Contact Information:
Dr. Steve Albrecht
DrSteve@DrSteveAlbrecht.com
www.DrSteveAlbrecht.com

ISBN -13: 978-1-960499-71-4

A Note About Future Editions of This Book:

We've tried to consider every possible safety and security event you're likely to encounter as an employee or as a supervisor. If there are items we need to add or issues we need to cover in future editions of this book, please send us an email at Book@mainstreamunlimited.com

TABLE OF CONTENTS

Important Contact Numbers and E-Mail Addresses

Write the name and contact information – work telephone number, cell number, or after-hours phone, and e-mail address – for as many of these safety and security stakeholders as you can:

My Office Address:

My Office Main Reception Number:

My City Police Department: 9-1-1 (plus the non-emergency number)

My County Sheriff's Office: 9-1-1 (plus the non-emergency number)

The Fire Department or Fire District for my area: 9-1-1 (plus the non-emergency number)

The State Police / Highway Patrol: 9-1-1 (plus the non-emergency number)

CEO/CAO's office:

City Manager or County Administrative Officer's office:

General Manager or Plant Manager:

Human Resources Director or Personnel Manager:

Security Director or Manager:

Security Office/Dispatcher (including afterhours/emergency number):

IT Director or Manager (including after-hours/emergency number):

Legal Counsel, County Counsel, or City Attorney:

Ethics Hotline/Ombudsman's Office:

Facilities Director or Manager (including after hours/emergency number):

Risk Management:

Safety Office/Safety Officer:

Communications Director or PIO:

Labor Relations or Union Representatives:

Employee Assistance Program (EAP) provider (if you have one):

My Department Director or Department Manager:

My direct supervisor, foreperson, or lead:

Alarm company for my building (if you have burglar alarm responsibility):

Building Landlord or Repair Contractor:

City or County Office of Emergency Management:

City or County Internal Emergency Operations Center:
The Emergency PA Announcements and Code Words we use:

The Floor Wardens for my building:

Locations of nearest AED machines, first-aid kits, earthquake kits:

Locations of nearest active shooter safe room or shelter-in-place room (or for weather emergencies):
Who do I contact for lost keys or my key card replacement?

Where are the Emergency Evacuation maps for my work area posted?

Where are any color-coded emergency clipboards?

Note to Myself:

I have read my organization's policies on:

- workplace violence
- fire and burglar alarm responses
- emergency evacuations
- first-aid
- safety hazards
- weather-related or earthquake responses
- ethics
- the protection of our Information Technology systems
- reporting fraud, theft, or embezzlement

QUICK START INFORMATION

Like with a manual for your laptop computer, desk, PC, smartphone, or an electronic device, sometimes it's best to jump right without having to get bogged down in the details. Use the following pages as your quick-start summary of this book. You can read and review the rest of the book later and as you need to, but for now, here's a fast look what you need to know:

Important Contact Numbers and E-Mail Addresses

Go to this section and jot down the phone numbers and e-mail addresses of the safety and security stakeholders for your organization.

Active Shooters and Workplace Violence Awareness and Response

Know the Run-Hide-Fight protocol for the rare but devastating possibility of an active shooter in your building. Watch either or both of the YouTube videos we discuss in this book.

Bomb, Telephone, and E-Mail Threats

Know that bomb threats are fake. Real bombers leave bombs; bomb threat makers leave bomb threats. Know who to tell and how to document any threats you receive over the phone, by e-mail, or in person.

Car Accidents or Personal Injury Events

Be ready to first aid at the level you have been trained. Be a good witness for the police or any other investigators and protect the scene if you can.

Car Thefts or Break-Ins

Park your locked and secured car in safe locations. Don't just leave your valuable items in the back seat or trunk; take them with you. Report unknown people trespassing in parking lots to Security or the police.

Dealing with Disturbances or Threatening People

Recognize the warning signs for violent people and stay clear of them. Be ready to call the police if a situation looks like it's getting out of hand. Use space and distance around angry or threatening people.

Dealing with Drug and Alcohol Users

Recognize the signs and behaviors of people under the influence of alcohol or drugs. Know they can be volatile, unstable, and threatening. Use space and distance to avoid them.

Domestic Violence in the Workplace

It's possible to see domestic violence issues cross over from home to work, involving a frightening personal issue in your own life or the lives of your co-workers. If it's your issue, have the courage to reach out for help from a trusted member of your safety and security stakeholder team. If it involves a co-worker, help them get help.

Facility Security Issues and Field Visits

It's easy to trade security for convenience. Help to keep all doors locked that need to be locked. Protect your hard keys, electronic key cards, and ID badges.

Fire, First Aid, and Medical Emergencies

Get trained in basic first aid; infant, child, and adult CPR; and how to use any Automated External Defibrillator (AED) devices in your facility. Be a good witness and tell the 9-1-1 dispatchers what they need to know.

Flu, Illnesses, and Pandemics

Stay home if you are sick or feeling sick with flu symptoms. Use your sick days appropriately. Follow governmental instructions if a pandemic develops.

Gang Problems and Gang Violence

Know that gang members can be violent, dangerous people, especially in groups. Report any gang activity, graffiti, or threats to your safety and security stakeholders or the police.

Homeless People and Trespassers

While only a small number of people experiencing homelessness are threatening, violent, or dangerous, many in this group have serious mental health or substance abuse issues that makes their behavior unpredictable. Pay attention to trespassers in and around your facility and be ready to call or the police.

Internal Threats, IT Security, and Economic Espionage

Follow the advice of your IT Department team when it comes to good password security and to avoid getting scammed. Report
co-workers who are engaging in unethical or illegal behaviors. The job you save just might be your own.

Panic Buttons

Know if you have panic buttons in your facility, where they ring to, and who responds. Press the button anytime you feel threatened, just like you would call 9-1-1 in a similar situation.

Robbery Prevention

Most robbers "case" the place they want to rob, so pay attention to anyone who looks like they are not there for legitimate reasons. Protect cash and things that have monetary value at all times. As soon as it's safe, call the police immediately after a robbery and be a good witness.

Self-Defense at Work

You have the right to reasonably protect yourself from violence. Make good decisions before situations escalate. Use space and distance, physical movement, and self-protection techniques to keep yourself safe from violent people.

Terrorism Awareness

Most acts of terrorism start with surveillance, trespassing, and information gathering. Pay attention to people who don't look like they are legitimate visitors to our facilities. Report what you see to your safety and security stakeholders, the police, or your nearest FBI office.

Vandalism, Tagging, and Graffiti

Report graffiti or tagging marks on our buildings as soon as you see them. A little of this type of vandalism now often leads to a lot more later.

Weather and Disaster Preparedness

Pay attention to local news reports, national weather forecasts, and get accurate information after an event happens. Make good decisions about going to work, staying safe at work, or staying safe at home.

INTRODUCTION

The times in which we live have given us a new reality about safety and security at work. Rising crime rates and the on-going threat of both terrorism and mass attacks by active shooters have heightened our responses to these significant issues. While it's never possible to predict violence or be completely safe from harm in our homes, neighborhoods, communities, libraries, schools, or workplaces, we can all become more aware and take certain important steps to respond, fight back, and harden our targets from any attack.

Safety and security in the workplace is every employee's responsibility, regardless of his or her title or position. You don't need permission to do the right and reasonable thing. Being safe at work will require you to give your full awareness, cooperation, support of your organization's policies, and in most cases, for you to use the power of your intuition. If you're ever at work and your intuitive voice asks you, "Should I call the police?" you already know the answer is yes. You have the right to reasonably protect yourself, get help from first responders without having to get permission from anyone, disengage from anyone who wants to cause you harm, and expect a response from your organization's safety and security stakeholders when you raise concerns.

We know that public and private-sector organizations and the employees who work for them in offices, factories, plants, campuses, and in the field, can lessen the likelihood of being targeted for crime or violence when they:

- follow approved safety and security-related policies and procedures;

- use all supplied security devices and report when they are not working correctly;

- remain vigilant inside and outside their facilities;

- pay attention to unusual situations or people;

- create Security Incident Reports and forward those to the safety and security stakeholders (listed below);

- get help from their bosses and other employees when they are confronted by threats, violence, or anything that may disrupt the safety of their workplace.

- and call for law enforcement or other first-responder help as soon as it appears necessary.

Our suggested audience for this security guide includes:

- All employees who work for public-sector or private-sector organizations and have face-to-face, over the counter, or over the phone contact with customers, clients, taxpayers, library patrons, ratepayers, vendors, visitors, or strangers.

- All executives, directors, managers, supervisors, and lead employees.

- Employees who do fieldwork, which includes contact with clients, customers, taxpayers, ratepayers, homeowners, caregivers, patients, or vendors.

- Employees who do home visits or provide patient care.

- Employees who interact over the phone, over the counter, or in the field with tenants, homeowners, or utility customers.

Employees with public-sector enforcement-related jobs, including:

- Code Compliance or Code Enforcement Officers
- Animal Control Officers
- Parking Enforcement Officers
- Building Inspectors
- Community Service Officers
- Court or Special Security Officers
- Fire Marshals
- Park Rangers
- Water or Electric Utility Rangers

Most bad things done by bad people start with them having some sort of a plan. The key to deterring potentially dangerous or violent people is to pay attention to any warning signs you see or hear and be ready to tell the safety and security stakeholders in your organization. If you work in the public or private sector, these people may include:

- The CEO/CAO's and his or her representatives
- The General Manager or Plant Manager
- The City Manager or County Administrative Officer
- Human Resources Director or Personnel Manager
- Security Director or Manager
- Police or Sheriff's Department IT Director
- Legal Counsel, County Counsel, or City Attorney
- Facilities Director or Manager
- Risk Management
- Safety Office or Safety Officer
- Communications Director or Public Information Officer
- Labor Relations or Union Representatives
- Elected or appointed officials (if you're a public-sector employee)
- Any Department Director or Department Manager
- Any supervisor, foreperson, or lead employee.

Our goals:

- to keep you safe, keep your facility safe, and help you continue to educate yourself and your colleagues on safety and security issues;

- to reinforce that you know your safety and security stakeholders (and how to contact them), preferably by name and not just by title;

- to protect your personal and work-related property and keep you and your information safe at your desk, workstation, or work area;

- to protect you from assault, robbery, or injury, at work or in the field;

- to help you know what to do during a likely emergency (a medical issue involving a co-worker) or an unlikely emergency (an active shooter situation);

- speaking of active shooters, to know what to do if this were ever to happen, either at work or out in public, using the Run-Hide-Fight protocol.

- to know the differences and how to recognize internal threats (a disgruntled current employee who sells company information or hacks the computer system) versus external threats (an ex-boyfriend who has made threats to harm his former girlfriend who works with you);

- to stay safe from robberies or assaults in your facility parking lots or garages.

You should know which first-responder agency answers 9-1-1 calls, first from calls made using any workplace landline and then, since we are all so attached to our mobile phones, from your cell phone. Using your cell to call out in an emergency may be faster and safer (if you need to hide out during an active shooter event, as one example), but it has its limitations too. During a large-scale emergency, the cell networks may be jammed with lots of calls and you may not be able to reach 9-1-1.

Further, with some facility or office landline phone systems, you may need to dial 9 first, to get an outside line, then 9-1-1. It can be tough to remember to do that under the stress of a life-threatening emergency. Landline phones offer the primary benefit of showing the dispatchers where the call is coming from (as long as the phone lines are trunked into that building). This certainly helps in an emergency, as does your ability to leave the phone off the hook, so the dispatchers can hear what's happening while you head to a safer place.

When using your cell phone to call, it's important to know who answers: is it your State Police or Highway Patrol? The local Police Department or Sheriff's Office? The local Fire Dispatch center? If the Highway Patrol answers, as is common in California, for example, there could be a delay while they transfer you to the right dispatch center, based in your region. If you have a choice between calling for 9-1-1 help on your cell or landline, choose the landline.

The leadership of your organization should be committed to providing you with a safe and secure workplace. They need to believe every suspicious security concern or safety incident is important because your overall safety is important. Your responsibility as an employee is to follow your policies, report incidents before they get out of control, and use the tools and resources given to you in this guidebook.

If you're a manager or a supervisor, you have a distinct and important set of duties beyond just managing your people, your team, or your department. You have a legal and ethical obligation to keep your employees as safe as possible while they work for you. There are obvious and hidden safety and security hazards in every workplace. We know you have a lot on your plate already, but the safety and security of your employees is the collective responsibility of you and all of the leaders in your organization.

We wrote this to be a living document, not something that gathers dust in your desk or workstation. We designed it for you to keep it updated and current, and even take it with you as you move along in your career.

Get the best use out of this multi-purpose information guide by personalizing it for your own needs. Fill in the blanks by asking the safety and security stakeholders in your organization for their help and support. Keep it updated if you change jobs or your key personnel change jobs. Store it in a safe and accessible place.

Refer to it regularly and make it work for you. Each section uses the same format:

Examples: The security or safety issue.

Important Information: Critical information for you to consider.

Action Steps: A more detailed look at what you need to know or do.

Employee Responsibilities: What you need to do versus what your boss or organization needs to do.

Supervisor Responsibilities: What you – if you're a supervisor or manager – or your bosses, or your organization needs to do to keep employees safe.

Reporting Procedures: Who to tell, why, when, and how.

As an employee of this organization, you should know that you are empowered to take any reasonable, legal, and appropriate steps to ensure your safety and the security of co-workers, visitors, vendors, or others who are on your properties or in your facilities for legitimate business reasons.

ACTIVE SHOOTERS AND WORKPLACE VIOLENCE AWARENESS AND RESPONSE

Examples:

A customer threatens to harm the office receptionist if she doesn't let him in to see a supervisor. A former employee or a job applicant comes into the workplace and demands to meet with the Human Resources Manager. An angry taxpayer or government client comes into an agency with a gun and threatens to shoot the employees. The current or former spouse or partner of an employee shows up to attack him or her. An ex-employee commits suicide at the office or factory location. A stranger targets the organization and its employees and shoots several people in the building for no known reason.

Important Information:

Active shooters and armed attackers coming into a workplace, K- 12 school, college or university, theater, or mall to kill people is devastating, horrific, chaotic, and fortunately, rarer than the media would like you to believe. There have certainly been more incidents in the last ten years, but the chances of you being injured or killed by a person with a gun are highly unlikely, especially if you don't work in a retail environment, in a healthcare setting, or at night, all of which tend to have higher risks of violence. (Men do the majority of these cases, but some women have been perpetrators as well. It's important not to generalize when it comes to these attackers or their motives, but for this subject, we will most often use the pronoun "he".)

Action Steps:

Besides following your organization's Workplace Violence Prevention Policy, the best thing you can do is familiarize yourself with the national protocol suggested by the Department of Homeland Security (DHS) known as Run-Hide-Fight. Every law enforcement agency in the US knows this approach and most all of their members have been trained to use it as their response to an armed perpetrator.

In order, the Run-Hide-Fight process means that if an armed attacker enters your worksite, your first best choice would be Run. Leave the building as safely and as quickly as possible to avoid the shooter. This means leaving your work items and only taking what you can carry, quickly and safely, with you (purse, backpack, wallet, cell phone). If you're on the ground floor and you're trapped in your workspace, you may have to break a window and climb out. The key is to move out quickly and get away from the danger, taking as many co-workers or others (visitors, customers, clients, patients, vendors) with you. As you leave, if you encounter any first-responders (police, firefighters, paramedics), be sure to give them your hard keys or electronic access key cards so they can move about the building safely and not get trapped in a locked hallway.

If getting out is not possible or safe, for your second preferred choice, you'll need to find a place to Hide out. This could be a break room, restroom, supervisor's office, storage room, file room, or even a closet. The key is to stay away from the shooter, lock or barricade the door as best as you can, stay out of the doorway (otherwise known as the "fatal funnel"), and wait for the arrival of the police. If you can safely call the police, using your cell phone, or better yet, a landline in the room, do so. Otherwise, turn off the lights, put as many heavy items as you can in front of the door, and stay quiet and as calm as you can, behind the relative safety of a locked or barricaded windowless room. We know very few of these shooters have shot through a closed door to kill people or have ever impersonated the police from the other side of the door. The police response is forthcoming, with the national average within five to ten minutes.

Your third and final (and necessary choice) is to Fight back against the attacker, using whatever objects (a pot of hot coffee or heavy books thrown at the attacker's face, chairs, desks or tables carried by several people) or actual or improvised weapons (knives, pepper spray, a fire extinguisher) to stop the attacker if he makes entry into your safe room.

Some key points: if the room you are hiding in cannot be locked or it opens from the outside, try to use your belt to tie up the door closing mechanism at the top (or tie two double doors together).

If you hear the fire alarm during a real active shooter situation, and you do not see flames or smell smoke, stay put. We've seen some attackers pull the fire alarm to get people into their kill zones. Scared employees or supervisors have pulled the fire alarm in their buildings in the mistaken belief that this will either expedite the police response or warn people to get out of the building. Pulling the fire alarm in a non-fire situation only creates more noise and adds to the chaos. Stay in your safe room until you're notified by the police or other first-responders that it's safe to evacuate.

If you have a key card that you wear around your neck or on your belt, remember to give it to the police or other first-responders, as you exit the building. We've seen too many examples of police officers and paramedics getting trapped in hallways where they don't have hard keys or key cards to get them into the interior of the building. Take this important step to give them your key card to speed their tactical response.

If you choose to leave your building during a real active shooter event, you may be able to drive or run to alternative evacuation locations located near your facility, like a church, store, mall, open government office, library, fire, police, or sheriff's station. The key is to get away to a safe location (you don't necessarily have to go inside one of these buildings), so you can connect with co-workers and wait out the event in safety.

Employee Responsibilities:

What we know about most active shooters is that before they decide to take lethal action, they tell someone near to them about their plan. This is called "leakage" and it happens when the bad people tell a co-worker, a friend, an acquaintance, or in the case of a planned school shooting, another student, what they are about to do. There are many reasons why they may do this but the important part is for you to have the courage to tell one of your organization's safety and security stakeholders what they have said to you, as safely and as soon as you can. Your information could save lives. The people you tell this disturbing information to could range from Human Resources to your boss to the local police. They should take the necessary next steps to confront the person who said they want to hurt others (without mentioning that it was you who told them), so they can redirect, stop, or arrest this person, depending on what they have leaked.

Don't wait until after a tragedy to come forward with important information that you have heard or overheard. Even gossip has some or a lot of truth to it. We know this leakage by potential attackers exists; it's up to you to tell the people in your organization so they can do something about it.

Many workplaces, K-12 schools, or college and university attackers have a target list, usually related to someone they hate, or who has disciplined or fired them, bullied them, shunned them or broke their hearts. It's common in many of these cases, where it is not a completely random attack designed to get a high casualty count, for these attackers to let some people live and seek to kill others on their lists. This suggests that how we treat people we work with or serve as customers, can go a long way toward not being on their target list. We can agree that you don't have to love or like every single person you work with or serve as a customer, but we need to treat everyone with dignity, patience, empathy, and respect because that's what professional people do in a professional, ethical workplace.

To help you reinforce the critical Run-Hide-Fight concepts, we suggest you watch one or both videos connected to the subject. The first is the DHS-created "Run-Hide-Fight" video co-created with the City of Houston, Texas. It's short and to the point. Here's a link to the City of Houston YouTube version:

https://www.youtube.com/watch?v=5VcSwejU2Do

We believe the second video option provides an even more effective message. It was created by the California State University system and it's an animated version of the Run-Hide-Fight approach. It may appeal to younger employees and is perhaps more empowering and less frightening than the DHS version. Both are useful and bear watching, at least once per year for yourself and then again as part of a staff meeting conversation about how to respond to an active shooter situation. Here's a link to the California State YouTube version:

https://www.youtube.com/watch?v=VUErkf3XEEs

Supervisor Responsibilities:

Use recent or previous workplace, school-based, or healthcare- related violence incidents as a teaching tool for your employees. You don't have to obsess over these events; use what happened as a way to stop the same thing from happening where you work. We can prevent this problem if we bring the possible solutions out into the light.

Pay attention to leakage from seemingly disturbed employees and to the reports you get from their equally-worried co-workers.

Don't ignore, brushoff, or delay your response to employees who have summoned up their courage, faced their fears of retaliation by the leaker, to come and have a confidential conversation with you.

Consider your Workplace Violence Prevention policy within the context of what you have heard and meet with your peer safety and security stakeholders as soon as possible to develop a response plan.

Work with your safety and security stakeholders to create emergency phrases to be used over the facility public address (PA) paging or notification systems. As an example, hospitals use color codes for various emergency events: Code Red (fire), Code Black (person with a gun), and Code Orange (chemical spill or gas leak). This type of color code system may be useful in a building with a lot of public traffic, so employees can focus on taking the necessary evacuation or shelter in place steps without scaring the public.

Any paging message should focus on what the issue is (fire, gas leak, earthquake, weather event, active shooter); where it is happening (location, building, floor); and what to do next (evacuate, shelter in place, move to a certain location, stage outside, or just flee, etc.). For events like real active shooters on the property, use the phrase "unusual incident" or "unusual event" to describe it, instead of saying "active shooter" over the PA. Train and remind all employees about your designated code words, since they won't work in an emergency if the employees won't remember them or don't know what to do.

Besides showing either or both Run-Hide-Fight videos, see if you can get senior management to agree to stage an annual "15- Minute Run-Hide Drill." This simply means that like staging a fire drill, an earthquake drill, or any other emergency drill, you set aside 15 minutes, once per year, at some point in the workday to ask your employees to demonstrate the two steps to the three-step active shooter response:

Leave the building for 15 minutes or hide out in some locked or barricaded part of the building for 15 minutes (their choice). If you walk around during the drill and can't see them outside or make entry into the rooms they have chosen to lockdown, then they have done the drill successfully.

That's it, and then they can go back to work. No need to demonstrate the third step, Fight, unless it was an actual active shooter emergency.

Sometimes senior management will balk at doing a Run-Hide drill because they think it's frivolous or a waste of time or worse yet, that it will somehow scare the employees. As a director, manager, or supervisor, your defense should be that we don't need to set an actual fire in the building to help employees know what to do in a real fire emergency. We still practice fire drills annually even though we assume every employee will know what to do if the building caught on fire or they smelled smoke or a gas leak.

Under stress and especially under life-threatening stress, most people revert to how they have been trained, told, or taught. This includes airline pilots and air traffic controllers, police officers and firefighters, paramedics, nurses, and doctors, who get extensive live, hands-on, stress-inducing training at the earliest stages of their careers and throughout them. This is why the Run-Hide portion of the overall Run-Hide-Fight response, is so important to practice at least once per year.

Reporting Procedures:

Workplace violence acts can be categorized into two primary behaviors: verbal or written threats and actual hands-on or violence using weapons. Both need to be reported and acted upon, but each may have its own level of intensity. As such, we can classify workplace violence threats or acts into three categories, with each having a corresponding response or set of decisions for the safety and security stakeholders to make:

Level 1: High Violence Potential – Person With a Weapon. Evacuate the area immediately and call 9-1-1 / law enforcement from a safe location. Provide information to the responding officers. Provide support or first aid until help arrives.

Level 2: Mid-Level Violence Potential – Deal with the person or the situation using help from HR, security, safety, IT, Facilities, Employee Assistance Program, or legal team members. Decide if you need to call law enforcement for a response or advice.

Level 3: Low to No Violence Potential – Deal with the person or situation using policies, Human Resources, security, or legal support.

BOMB, PHONE AND EMAIL THREATS

Examples:

A bomb threat comes to your headquarters or office facility from a phone call, an e-mail message, a voice message left on an employee's telephone or for a department, or employees discover or learn of a suspicious package in or near their facility. A phone threat comes in where the caller threatens to "shoot up the place," "go postal," or kill everyone in the building with a gun or a bomb. An e-mail threat comes in from a known or unknown person, threatening a mass attack or a shooting.

Important Information:

The simple fact is that most real bombers in the U.S. do not make bomb threats. Most people who make bomb threats are either mentally ill, seeking revenge, or simply want to disrupt the operations of the business they threaten. Therefore, we will not automatically evacuate the facility based solely on a bomb threat and without the discovery of a real or suspected bomb device. People who do ultimately plant bombs or try to detonate them do not warn their intended targets. They want the bomb to go off, so the existence of a bomb threat itself means a bomb in the building is highly unlikely.

Most workplace violence threats that come in via e-mail are hoaxes as well, especially if the supposed shooter does not identify himself in either the e-mail address (like John.Smith@example.com). It's usually sent by someone using an anonymous e-mail address because he or she doesn't want to be identified, caught, and prosecuted. People who make workplace violence threats using their real e-mail addresses either don't care about the consequences of their actions, want people to be scared and know who scared them, or are so mentally ill that they don't think or care about covering their tracks. They tend to be much more problematic than anonymous threateners.

It's important to report any e-mail threats to your safety and security stakeholders as soon as you receive them. There are threat assessment and threat management steps we can take to catch, deter, or stop these people once we identify them.

Action Steps:

The three most important responses to bomb threats: gather as much data as possible from the person making the bomb threat (usually over the telephone); call law enforcement immediately after this conversation; and follow their instructions upon their arrival.

The four most important responses to phone or e-mail threats mentioning mass shootings or other forms of workplace violence: notify your boss or another safety and security stakeholder; get as much information from the caller as you can; protect the electronic evidence (save any recorded voicemail messages, print out and take a screenshot of any texts or e-mails); discuss whether you need to call the police or manage the situation using your internal resources.

Employee Responsibilities:

If you work in a reception area, have a copy of your organization's Bomb/Telephone/E-Mail Threat Checklist near your telephone, or stored in a discreet place you can remember under stress.

If a bomb threat or a workplace violence threat comes in via a phone call, be a good witness and a better listener. The information you provide (as shown on your Check List) can help the police catch the person.

After a bomb threat phone call, notify your supervisor immediately (and quietly) what has just happened. You or your supervisor should call law enforcement via 9-1-1 immediately. The police may or may not respond and if they do arrive, they may or may not order an evacuation. This doesn't mean they don't care about your safety, just that if they have experience managing bomb threats, they will investigate before they evacuate.

You may be called upon, by the police, to help them search for a suspicious object. This is not designed to frighten you or make you touch or handle a suspected bomb. It may simply be because you know the facility better than the first responders and can tell them what should or should not be there, what looks out of place, what was just delivered or dropped off, etc. Tell law enforcement if any deliveries were made to coincide with the arrival of the suspicious package.

If you find any suspicious package or device before their arrival,
don't touch it in any way.

Block off the area and warn others to leave the facility immediately, saying only, "We need to evacuate the building now."

If you find a suspicious device before the arrival of law enforcement, do not use your cell phone anywhere near it. Leave the building immediately before calling 9-1-1.

Supervisor Responsibilities:

Make sure all public-contact employees have copies of a Bomb/ Telephone/E-Mail Threat Check List near their landline phones. (You can create one using examples and templates from the Internet.) Discuss how to fill out this form and how to be a good witness and listener.

Try to keep all employees as calm as possible and tell them not to make any comments that could frighten visitors or other staffers before law enforcement arrives.

Remember that most bomb threateners make highly unrealistic, larger than life threats. Saying, "I'm gonna take down the whole building!" would require a huge truck and a huge bomb, not a likely possibility.

The discovery of any suspicious package or device, with or without a bomb threat, should cause you to put your facility evacuation plans into action.

But remember that we won't necessarily evacuate the building just because we received a bomb threat. Every situation and each incident is different and must be managed on a case-by-case basis, not a "one size fits all" basis.

If you are told to evacuate, get as far from the building as possible (including getting into your car and driving away). Do not use your cell phone within a quarter-mile of the building.

Reporting Procedures:

Pay attention to other local incidents of bomb threats in your community. These cases often have a copycat nature to them. Giving as much information to the police as possible can help them develop a pattern of behavior for the threatener and help them make an arrest.

Put a copy of your Bomb, Telephone, or E-Mail Threat Form here.

CAR ACCIDENTS OR PERSONAL INJURY EVENTS

Examples:

A car accident in our employee parking lot, on the street near our facilities, or one of our employees is involved in a crash with his or her work/fleet or personal vehicle. A slip-and-fall accident in our offices or on the adjacent sidewalks. An employee is injured while working in our plant, factory, or yard.

Important Information:

As either an employee or supervisor, you have two primary goals: help with any serious medical injuries by calling 9-1-1 for an ambulance/paramedic response and make sure the accident doesn't get worse (for example, by blocking off on-coming traffic into the parking lot).

If you get into a car accident while working, first pull to a safe side of the street or highway. Check for injuries and if there are none, exchange insurance information with the other driver. Do not admit fault or argue about who is at fault. If either party says he or she was injured, call 9-1-1 and request an ambulance. You will want to get the names of all drivers and passengers, vehicle information (plates, model, etc.), and if possible, use your cell phone to take pictures of the damage on both cars. Report this to your supervisor by phone or as soon as you return to work.

The best way to avoid an accident while driving a company or agency car, or driving your own car while on company or agency business, is to pay careful attention to how you drive and where you're driving, especially when other drivers around don't do much of either. Too many drivers create car accidents by speeding, following too closely, not signaling for lane changes, and texting or looking at their phones as they drive.

If you drive for any reason on behalf of your organization, you'll need to follow a strict policy of no texting while driving and always using the hands-free option to make or receive calls.

Action Steps:

The key to litigation protection in an accident situation is to document what you have seen, said, or done. When it's safe to do so, write down what you saw, what others told you, or what others told you they saw or heard. Say nothing about who was at fault in the accident. Do not discuss any potential liability issues involving our facilities, cars, or our property, e.g., "I knew we should have put a stop sign there."

Employee Responsibilities:

If you witness a car accident or other personal injury event, start thinking about getting emergency help enroute. Have your cell phone ready as you approach the scene (as long as it's safe to do so).

If it's clear from the injuries or what the parties tell you that medical help is needed, dial 9-1-1, give the location or address, and describe the situation in detail: "We have a two-car accident, involving three adults, one who looks like he has a head injury."

Provide basic first aid or CPR (only if you have been trained) until the paramedics arrive and take over. Assist the first responders by keeping other people clear of the scene.

Don't move or touch any potential pieces of evidence for investigators. This can include pieces of car parts, broken machinery, damaged equipment, ropes, belts, chains, tools, or safety guards. For a serious-injury car accident, the local police or sheriff's department will often send specially trained traffic officers to investigate what happened. For serious-injury events involving employees, contractors, or subcontractors, it's likely state and/or federal OSHA inspectors and investigators will respond. Leave the accident scene just as it was.

If you have witnessed a traumatic incident, consider calling the Employee Assistance Program for debriefing and support. If you feel your work performance is being hurt by what you experienced, discuss it with your supervisor, get EAP help, and take the time you need to recover.

Supervisor Responsibilities:

When calling 9-1-1 for a car or other accident, describe the situation accurately, giving the ages, genders, and possible injuries of the victims. This will help the first responders prepare while enroute.

Keep bystanders and others away from the scene of the accident until the police arrive. Don't let anyone touch or remove any potential evidence.

Gather as much information as possible, including names, addresses, and phone numbers, of victims and witnesses. The best time to get their statement is immediately and at the scene. Note the time, weather, lighting conditions, road conditions, any construction, visibility, and any object or situation that may have led to the accident.

Remember, the report you create for this incident may last for years and be the subject of many reviews by insurance companies, investigators, attorneys, judges, or juries. Write a complete account of what occurred, with captions for your photos.

Reporting Procedures:

Complete your Fleet Accident Report form. (Create one using examples or templates from the Internet.)

CAR THEFTS OR BREAK INS

Examples:

Your personal or work car is broken into, damaged, or vandalized in the parking lot or parking garage at or near your worksite. Your personal or work car is broken into while you are parked at a field location during working hours.

Important Information:

Annually, more cars are broken into than are stolen each year. The reasons are obvious: too many people leave items in their cars that thieves want (money, cell phones, checkbooks, tools, laptops, clothing, luggage, computer bags, purses, backpacks, wallets, and even guns); it's easy to break a window or use a crowbar to pry open the trunk (instead of having to defeat a car alarm system); it's fast; and in many states, the criminal penalties for breaking into a car are less when compared to stealing the car. You need to take steps to make sure nothing is valuable or visible in your car. Hiding things in your trunk, glove box, in the center console, or under the seat is not enough. If it's valuable, leave it at home or take it with you when you lock up your car.

Action Steps:

Keeping your car safe from a break-in starts with paying close attention to where you park it. A covered parking garage may not be a good choice when compared to parking on the street in front of your office (as long as you can avoid a parking citation).

Parking garages are rarely patrolled by security guards (and never visited by police officers, unless they are called there for a crime). Camera systems are not always commonly installed in parking garages either. The lighting is often poor. Thieves know they usually have time to choose the car they want to burglarize.

If a parking attendant is working in a booth, park as close to that person as you can. Avoid parking far from the staircases or elevators; you want lots of people to be walking by your car all day.
If you have to take a work trip, avoid leaving your car overnight in a parking garage that has no security guards. Pay the extra money for valet parking, since you can at least hope that your car will be more visible to the valet attendants.

Employee Responsibilities:

Pay careful attention to your choices when it comes to parking your car in the field. Note the reputation of the neighborhood. Is it known for a lot of car burglaries? Are certain garages or parking lots known to be safer than others, based on the design or the employees working there? How is the lighting? How is the access to the stairs, elevators, or street?

Leave nothing that can be stolen in a visible location inside your car or your trunk. This includes your vehicle registration (keep it in your purse or wallet, not the glove box). Even the spare change you keep in a cup in your cup holder is worth stealing to some crooks. Empty out your car and don't leave clothes going to or from the dry cleaners, winter jackets, any electronics, or any personal or company information (files, fiduciary instruments) in your car. Take important or expensive things (tablets, laptops, day planners, checkbooks, phones) with you when you go to meetings, hotels, the airport, coffee shops, or restaurants.

Program the upper console of your car to serve as your garage door remote. Don't leave your garage remote device in your car. If the crook discovers your personal address from your insurance or registration card and has your remote, he can go to your house, and burglarize it, knowing you're not there.

Supervisor Responsibilities:

Remind all employees who travel or work in the field to pay careful attention to where and when they park their personal or work vehicles. Monitor reports of break-ins in any company-owned or operated parking lots or garages. If you have security officers, deploy them to the parking garage or lot to patrol more often or provide escorts to employees going to their cars at night.

Reporting Procedures:

Report all break-ins to the local police or sheriff's department. Ask them to take a report, even if it's only over the phone or online.

Most law enforcement agencies don't have the time or the personnel to send an officer or a deputy to take photos, look for clues, or "dust for fingerprints" (like we see them do on TV).

Chances are slim you will get your property back unless the cops happen to come across a prolific car burglar and recover your things along with a lot of other stuff. You'll need a police report for your organization's insurance company or your own. A lot of police reports coming from one location may tell the local police or sheriff's department where they need to start targeting their extra surveillance or patrol efforts.

DEALING WITH DISTURBANCES OR THREATENING PEOPLE

Examples:

A taxpayer comes into the Tax Collector's office to complain about a fee. The conversation escalates to where this person threatens the staff with harm. A mental health client becomes angry while in an interview room with a therapist. A maintenance employee is threatened by a stranger while painting over graffiti.

Important Information:

The bad news is that verbal threats are frightening and can affect your work performance and that of your co-workers. The good news is that most verbal threats, with a few important exceptions, are mostly just about one person trying to scare another.

Research into violence suggests that many people make threats; few people carry them out. The exceptions to this idea come when the victim and the threatener have had some kind of dating/ marriage relationship, or the suspect has a history of violence, mental illness, or gang membership.

There is a difference between someone who is angry with you or the situation and someone who is threatening you. You should be concerned about every threat made to you, your facility, and your organization. Threats, with some necessary elements to establish the crime, are illegal, under most state Penal Codes. You have the right, as a victim of a threat, to make a police report. It's a felony to threaten employees with injury or death so that they believe it's possible, and are afraid to work, answer the phone, go outside, etc., even if the threatener did not really mean the threat. Law enforcement will use threat statutes in cases involving workplace violence threats to an employee or the worksite, gang intimidation, stalking, and domestic violence situations.

As an employee, you have many reasonable options when dealing with threatening people. When someone threatens you at work, he or she threatens all of us. You have a right to work in an
environment that is free from threats. You also have a duty as an employee to tell your supervisor, so he or she can respond – often using support from other safety and security stakeholders.

Employee Responsibilities:

<u>Customer, Client, Visitor, Taxpayer, Ratepayer, Stranger Complaints:</u>

Use space, distance, and barriers (like desks,

countertops, glass windows, etc.) to your advantage, to help keep people out of your personal space and away from touching, hitting, or harming you.

Keep in mind that for most people, the situation they're angry about doesn't involve you personally. They're not always mad at you, but mostly at what you represent (an authority figure, someone they believe who has control over their home or life, is causing them financial pain, etc.).

Use a "venting and validation" process. Let them talk or yell, without arguing back. Try to remain as quiet as you can while they vent, nodding or taking notes as you feel it may help to show you're listening and you're trying to solve their issues.

The "validation" step starts when you can acknowledge they're angry. Use phrases like: "I hear you. I can see that you're upset. I understand your concerns. I'm sorry this has happened to you.
You could be right. I'll try to help you as best as I can." Apologizing for their issue doesn't mean we are at fault, just that you see this person is upset and you're trying to show empathy.

If the person demands to speak to your supervisor, suggest he or she leaves a message, calls back later, makes an appointment, or returns later. This time gap can help the responding supervisor to prepare for this subsequent phone call or meeting, by talking to you or researching the situation that led to this person's anger.

Try hard to keep your body language as neutral as possible. Rolling your eyes, crossing your arms, looking at your watch, or sighing loudly will only make them angrier. Model appropriate neutral body language on your part. Know that there may be cultural differences in the body language, tone, gestures, and words that you and the other person use.

Keep the condescension out of your voice and body language. No adult likes to be spoken down to or as if he or she were a child.

Keep your voice low and don't escalate to match the threatener's tone if he or she is getting loud.

Change the ratios of confrontation. When you feel you need help in the situation, get immediate support from a co-worker or a supervisor.

Customer, Client, Visitor, Taxpayer, Ratepayer, Stranger Threats:

If the situation escalates to where you feel afraid for your safety, disengage immediately, go to a safe place, and call 9-1-1.
Describe the person's behavior, not by using labels ("He's crazy!"), but by talking about what he or she is doing that is so threatening and why you need a police response.

Once the person has left, or the police have responded, and the emotional temperature has decreased enough for you to think clearly, write down exactly what happened in a Security Incident Report. Note the time, date, the person's name (if you know it), who witnessed the event, what the threatener said, and how you responded. If the police were called, get the responding officer's name and ID number and a case number for the incident.

Safety in Interviewing Rooms:

Every situation is different when dealing with people who may get angry and make threats during interviews. Even if they initially feel you're there to help them, they may still lose control of their emotions. Meeting with people in small rooms can cause stress for all parties. Here are some guidelines for Interview Room dynamics:

Use the person's past history with you and your co-workers as a good measure of how he or she might act when you meet. A good predictor of future bad behavior is past bad behavior. If the person has been relatively cooperative in the past, chances are that will continue. If the person has been angry and difficult in the past, chances are good you may see that behavior again.

Have the right number of people in the room to support you. More than three employees are probably one too many, but working alone might not be safe either. If this person has had angry experiences with you in the past, ask your boss or a colleague to sit in with you. (If that becomes necessary, decide if you should use a larger conference room or a meeting room instead of a small interview room with the client.)

Position yourself so that you sit with your back to the far wall and the client sits closest to the door. This sounds wrong and counterintuitive, but the fact is, angry people do not like to see anything, including you, blocking their escape path. If they act up and want to leave, you do not want to be in their way. The best practices for any high-stress or high-stakes interview is to sit "door neutral," meaning you and the client are at equal measurements to the exit door.

If you find yourself alone in a room with this person who makes a threat of harm, tell him or her, "I can't help you if you threaten me. This meeting is over. Please leave."

If the person refuses, you have to decide if you want to leave yourself, activate your personal panic alarm (if you've been given one), press an in-room panic button (if one has been installed), yell for help to a co-worker, or dial for help (from a co-worker, supervisor, or police, using the telephone in the interview room).

Supervisor Responsibilities:

Monitor the history and contacts with all clients who need to meet with your employees to see if you need to get involved. Respect their ability, but don't let situations deteriorate into shouting, threats, or violence without your intervention.

Take the lead and sit in on any Interview Room encounters where you have a feeling that the meeting will not go smoothly. Better to be in the room already, supporting your employee, than have to come running from your office.

In some instances, simply arriving on the scene and introducing yourself as an authority figure will cause the other person to calm down.

If you feel the situation is escalating, be firm and say, "You can't speak to our employees in that way. We want to treat you with courtesy and respect. You have to do the same. We can't help you if you don't cooperate. We'll need to reschedule this meeting at another time."

Know that some people will play the role of "professional victim" and that no idea or solution you give them will ever solve their problems. Set limits on what you will do for these types of people. Don't over-promise. You can frustrate yourself by coming up with too many solutions for people who simply enjoy arguing, conflict, and confrontation.

Filling out the Bomb, Telephone, or E-Mail Threat Form may be useful for situations involving threats by clients. Encourage your employees to use it for workplace threats. Assist them in documenting the threatening event, to help you or law enforcement to investigate the behavior.

Since the best indicator of future behavior is past behavior, prepare yourself and your employees for any subsequent encounters with the threatener. This may include having the threatener work only by telephone appointments, meeting with you instead of the employee, or having a police or security representative at the meeting.

For certain high-risk clients, patients, or taxpayers who continually engage in disruptive or threatening behaviors with staff during meetings, it may be useful for you to convene a discussion with your safety and security stakeholders to discuss the best methods to handle these people, still provide necessary services to them, but to keep your staff safe while doing so.

Reporting Procedures:

Share information with your colleagues about difficult, entitled, or threatening people you all deal with. Discuss what seems to work best when meeting with these people. Keep your supervisors informed as to when you may need help in managing these meetings.

DEALING WITH DRUG AND ALCOHOL USERS

While working in the field, you see a woman staggering across the parking lot. She is holding a liquor bottle, cursing, and yelling at everyone and no one. She is missing one shoe and appears to have a serious cut over her eye from a previous fall. Is this a police matter or a medical concern? (The answer is both.)

Important Information:

While alcoholic beverages are certainly legal and part of our national fabric (interrelated to sporting events, commercial sponsorships, holidays, etc.), the problem comes when the alcohol user becomes the abuser.

The impact of alcohol abuse in our society is staggering: over 50 percent of all automobile injuries and fatalities involve alcohol, prescription, or illegal drugs, and it plays a large part in domestic violence, child abuse, suicides, and violent crimes. The health risks due to the chronic use of drugs or alcohol include liver, kidney, lung, and pancreas diseases; several forms of cancer; stomach ulcers; diabetes; and brain injuries. Alcohol and drug abuse and related overdose deaths exist at every level in society and no city, county, or neighborhood is immune.

We will briefly discuss employees who are impaired at work and spend more time on people you may encounter as you do your work in field or public-contact situations.

Employees who use illegal drugs or alcohol at work, abuse prescription drugs, or come to work under the influence of drugs or alcohol put us all at risk of injuries or deaths if they operate vehicles, trucks, dangerous equipment, or machinery. Their drug and alcohol behavior can cause conflicts, create opportunities for theft or damage, hurt the retention of sober employees, create a bad reputation in the business community, and generally just drive down morale.

If you're an employee, you don't need to spy on your co-workers or become a tattletale. But you do have to have the courage to report to your boss or Human Resources what you see when it comes to your suspicions about drug and alcohol behavior.

The most common drugs of abuse include:

Marijuana – this naturally-grown depressant and hallucinogenic substance is known to cause anxiety attacks and long-term depression in heavy users.

Methamphetamine – this man-made chemical stimulant, made in powder form, causes mood swings, sleep disturbances, organ and brain damage, and irrational, paranoid, or even violent behavior in chronic users.

Cocaine – this naturally-grown (from the coca plant) and chemically-processed stimulant powder causes nasal damage, heart rhythm problems, and mood swings in nearly all users.

Opiates – including heroin, morphine, pain pills (Vicodin, OxyContin, Codeine), and fentanyl (synthetic opiates), these depressive substances are highly addictive, even after a few doses.

Depressants – this includes the abuse of anti-depressants and anti-anxiety pills, sleep aids, and similarly physician-prescribed pharmaceuticals. The issue is not the use of these drugs (under appropriate medicinal circumstances), but their abuse.

Other common street drugs – PCP or Ketamine; LSD, Ecstasy or MDMA tablets; "bath salts" and "spice"; inhaling spray paints, thinners, or solvents. Because of questionable purity and enormous toxicity, using these substances can cause brain damage, irrational behavior, and even sudden death.

If you do any of your work in the field, you may come across people under the influence and impaired by any of the above substances. Know that it's illegal for people to be drunk in public or under the influence of drugs in a public place, especially if that impairment makes them a danger to themselves, a danger to others, or unable to care for their safety.

When in doubt about irrational people and their level

of sobriety, stay clear of them and pay attention to your safety. Call the police if they're having behavior problems or they want to hurt themselves or others. Call paramedics if the person is having medical issues that seem severe enough that they need a medical evaluation. (This is most common when opiate users overdose and pass out in public places like parks, restrooms, libraries, or on the street.)

Not all people under the influence of drugs or alcohol are violent, but many can become agitated if they feel provoked, frustrated, prevented from doing something, or from getting their way. Some of these people use their intoxication as their excuse for hurting someone or even themselves. They may have rapid mood swings, going from tears to threats to anger to apologies, all in a few minutes. Use simple language, ask simple questions, and speak in low tones. Keep your distance (no closer than 10 or so feet away) and be ready to put barriers between you and the person (desks, locked doors, fences, railings, mailboxes, fire hydrants, picnic tables, etc.). Disengage if you feel threatened and wait for the police to arrive from a safe location.

Action Steps:

Use your intuition to size up the level of sobriety for strangers you encounter at work, in the field, or in the streets. Most of us know what it's like to have had a bit too much to drink, so we can often recognize the signs and symptoms of alcohol impairment. People under the influence of stimulant drugs tend to be aggressive and confrontational. People under the influence of depressant drugs tend to be more passive or even lethargic. People in withdrawal from either type of drug can be agitated and unpredictable. Be careful around anyone who seems out of control.

Employee Responsibilities:

Certain locations on or near our facilities can become hangouts for chronic drug and alcohol users (libraries, adjacent parks, parking lots, open areas, etc.). Call the police when you see people congregating, fighting, or causing problems in these areas and break this pattern before it develops.

If you must make contact with suspected drug and alcohol users, get help from a co-worker or a supervisor. Change the ratio of the confrontation, so that there are more people on your side as you talk to the person. You don't want to give off a menacing or overly aggressive impression, but you do want additional staff support and other witnesses.

Decide if the person you are dealing with can simply be asked, politely, to leave the facility, or if you need to call the police, or if his or her problem is medical. In some instances, the police may arrive and take the person to a mental health facility for an examination; in others, the fire department or EMTs may take the person to a hospital for treatment. While you don't always need to speak to your supervisor first as to which of these options to choose, it may help to have a brief group discussion as to the best choice.

Sometimes, you may have a good rapport, previous experience, or a good connection with a suspected drug or alcohol abuser. You may be able to talk to this person in a way that keeps him or her calm and relatively rational. In other situations, nothing you do or say will satisfy this person. Keep in mind that what might have worked well in the past, like asking the person to leave, might suddenly become the triggering event for an argument or a fight now. Use your intuition and know when to talk and when to leave or get help.

Supervisor Responsibilities:

If you're a manager or a supervisor, you have to pay attention to the signs of impairment in your employees. Trust your eyes and ears, your nose, and your intuition. Get help from a peer supervisor or your boss, or Human Resources when you suspect impairment in any employee, not just those working for you. Use the substance abuse testing protocols designed by your Human Resources Department, to treat all employees legally and fairly, but assertively, if you suspect impairment.

Monitor the work area and the facility perimeters for the continued presence of drug and alcohol-addicted people. Some of these people have a magnetic connection to a public, governmental facility because they feel that they should be able to receive some sort of assistance, money, support, or tell their story to someone who will listen. Try to discourage these types of interactions, since the more you allow them to engage with you or your staff, the worse it can get. When they are under the influence, some of these people feel quite entitled and that the "government" owes them something. If they don't get "it," their behavior can turn threatening or violent.

Allow your employees to trust their intuition when it comes to dealing with drug or alcohol users. Don't force them into a position where they have to justify calling for the police or an ambulance. It's possible some employees have a drug or alcohol history in their past, which makes them quite capable of accurately assessing the behavior of the users they encounter.

Use the power of your authority when dealing with some drug and alcohol users. It's possible that even though they may verbally abuse your staff, they may respond more favorably to you if they see you as an authority figure or boss. When in doubt, disengage, make sure your employees are in a safe place, get away from the person, and call 9-1-1 for police help. Not surprisingly, the police usually have significant experience dealing with specific drug and alcohol abusers, often over many years of their drug or alcohol use. As such, they will often know them by name and can handle the contact in a way that de-escalates the potential for violence and by removing them from the area.

Reporting Procedures:

You can talk to any of your safety and security stakeholders if you have concerns about drug or alcohol use by one of your co- workers. You can also get confidential help from a variety of resources inside or outside your organization if you are struggling with drug or alcohol dependence yourself. This includes your HR Department, your Employee Assistance Program provider, Alcoholics Anonymous or Narcotics Anonymous chapters in your community, your medical doctor, a qualified addiction counselor, or a mental health clinician.

DOMESTIC VIOLENCE IN THE WORKPLACE

Examples:

An employee comes to the Human Resources office, shaken and injured from a fight with her husband. An employee gets threatening phone calls from his or her ex-spouse or partner. An employee starts being stalked by a vendor, who calls the office repeatedly or comes by regularly. The ex-spouse of an employee violates a Temporary Restraining Order (TRO).

Important Information:

Domestic violence becomes a workplace issue when it affects the safety, performance, and productivity of our employees. While we don't want to pry into an employee's personal life, we will when off-the-job domestic violence arrives at work in the form of threats, civil order violations, or assaults. There is much emotional energy around these difficult issues and they can put many lives at risk. Your organization can work in partnership with law enforcement agencies, domestic violence assistance agencies, support groups, shelters, and our Employee Assistance Program (EAP) to provide safety solutions to victim-employees.

Employee Responsibilities:

Employee-Victim:

If you are a victim of domestic violence, you have people who care about you and resources in your workplace that can help you break the cycle of violence. These include your Human Resources Department, your Security Department (if you have that function), your Employee Assistance Program provider, your supervisor, a Department Director, or a member of law enforcement. You can also call the 24/7 National Domestic Violence hotline at 800-799-7233.

If you have a civil order, known as a stay-away order, an Emergency Protective Order (EPO), or a Temporary Restraining Order (TRO) and you have any concerns that the restrained person may come to work and threaten or harm you or others, you must tell your employer about it. We can't fix what we don't know about. Talk to your boss, your boss's boss, another manager or supervisor you trust, and especially your HR Department. They can work as a team to move you to a safer part of the building, put you in another facility, put you on temporary leave, and help you connect with domestic violence support agencies or groups who can help you stay safe. The time to discuss the situation is not when the suspect in the front lobby of your building, looking for you.

Employee-Witnesses:

If you work in a taxpayer or public-contact job, you may encounter situations involving a person seeking help who has been victimized by domestic violence. The victim can be an adult male or female fearful of his or her same-sex partner, a high school girl, an adult female, or a pregnant woman (studies tell us that the leading cause of non-medical deaths for pregnant women is homicide). No matter the victim, these people are in need.

However, sometimes, because of the emotionality of the situation, they are too scared, angry, or preoccupied to want our help.

Nonetheless, we have an obligation to help these people by making calls for police, medical, or victim advocacy services when we come across them. Law enforcement officers are familiar with the dynamics (and their legal requirements, which can vary by agency) in these situations, so they are the best choice to call and help intervene.

If the victim is alone and the suspect is not in the area but may return, you may want to bring the victim into the lobby of your office, call 9-1-1, and have him/her wait for the police to arrive. Lock the main facility door and notify your supervisor immediately.

Call paramedics if you think they need to assess the victim for any injuries. Do this even if the victim refuses medical treatment; some injuries can cause shock and others, like after being choked, are actually more serious than they first appear (internal bleeding, breathing problems, brain damage). When in doubt, get medical help.

Get the victim's name, address, and telephone number. Ask the person if you can call anyone to assist with the situation.

Help the responding police by describing how you became involved in the situation and what, if anything, you know about the suspect.

If the suspect is still with the victim, and the conflict is continuing, call 9-1-1 from a safe place, preferably inside your facility with the door locked.

Do not try to intervene to save the victim, unless you have the skills to do so. These situations escalate and worsen quickly and you could be victimized, assaulted, or even killed trying to help. Let the police do their job. You can't help the victim if you get injured as well.

If the suspect flees and the victim is still there, try to protect the crime scene until the police arrive. This may include torn clothing, bloodstains, weapons, etc.

Give the police a description of the suspect and the exact location of the incident. Be a good witness and tell the dispatcher about any weapons, injuries, etc., that you see.

Supervisor Responsibilities:

If an employee tells you he or she has a civil protection order – most often called a Temporary Restraining Order (TRO) or Emergency Protective Order (EPO) – against another person due to domestic violence, ask to see a copy of the order.
Verify that the order is valid (it has not expired) and it

has been served (given to the restrained person and filed with the court). If neither of these two conditions is met, the protection order may not be in force. (Many permanent restraining orders cover a three-year time span.)

If the order is valid, ask the employee how certain he or she feels the person will violate the order in the workplace. In some situations, the person has never violated the order; in others, it's a frequent event.

If the employee feels the person could or has violated the order, ask what accommodations you might need to make the workplace safer for all involved. This could include a temporary job transfer to a new location, additional security measures, police involvement, counseling, etc.

Once the employee has given you his or her perspective, contact your supervisor and Human Resources immediately, to discuss the issues. HR or Security may ask the employee for the restrained person's photo, but it should not get posted around the facility for privacy reasons.

Tell the employee he or she should call the police and make a report every time the person violates the no-contact terms of the order. This is critical. The protective order is worthless if the employee does not enforce it or worse, enforces it sporadically and only if the person becomes unreasonable or threatening. Any contact (phone, e-mail, text, a letter left on the victim's car, etc.) means he or she should make a police report.
These situations demand discretion and paying attention to privacy and confidentiality concerns. So

as not to get sued for invasion of privacy or damage to a person's reputation, keep the circulation of the suspect's photo and information about the protection order on a need-to-know group of safety and security stakeholders or designated employees. This should include other facility supervisors and employees who serve reception or public counter functions.

Keep this information on a need-to-know basis. Only tell those employees, who may have the most opportunity to see the person to call or notify you if possible, or call 9-1-1 immediately to report the arrival of the suspect and the violation of the civil order.
If the restrained party enters the facility, you may have to intervene on behalf of your (victim) employee. Tell your employee to leave the room and call the police. Tell the person you know about the restraining order and that he or she will have to leave immediately.

If the situation escalates, disengage, go (with the other employees) to a safe location, verify someone has called 9-1-1, and wait for the arrival of the police.

Reporting Procedures:

There are many resources to help employees who have domestic violence issues. States are now changing their labor laws to make it illegal to fire employees who reveal they have a domestic violence issue. In California, as one example, employers are also expected to create a workplace safety plan for the employee who tells them about their domestic violence situation.

FACILITY SECURITY ISSUES AND FIELD VISITS

Examples:

Broken door locks; unlocked facility doors after-hours; suspicious people in the area, or theft of personal or work property; bee swarms; found narcotics or syringes at the library; stolen property; abandoned, stolen, or stripped vehicles; lost children.

Important Information:

Broken office door locks and broken exterior lights seem like small things, but when left unrepaired, they can allow criminals and others to enter our facilities or vandalize our properties. Make it a habit to use the small security devices: desk and file drawer locks, storage door locks, window locks, gate locks, exterior lights, etc. to keep people out of our facilities. Use our facility's shredders to make sure that no employee, customer, or vendor data is thrown into office trashcans. Complete an End-of-the-Day Security Checklist each working day.

As you have read throughout this book, it makes good security sense to trust your instincts. If the situation in the office or the field doesn't feel right, don't go forward into it. Disengage and get help, up to and including calling 9-1-1 for a law enforcement response. If you see people loitering or looking like they're about to fight or steal, don't hesitate to call 9-1-1 and describe what you're seeing.

Action Steps:

Decide if the assistance issue is primarily a law enforcement problem, a fire department problem, something that can be handled by the leadership team, along with one of our vendors, or an incident that should involve a city or county agency (Water and Power, Public Works, Animal Control, etc.). Some of the examples listed above are emergency situations, which will require a 9-1-1 call and some are not. For those that are not, remember to call the non-emergency numbers for law enforcement or related agencies, so as not to tie up the lines for real emergencies.

When in doubt about who to call, consult your organizational phone lists in your facility or look online for the number of the appropriate governmental agency or vendor (locksmith, plumber, HVAC repair specialist, exterminator, etc.) in your area.

Don't ever think that the police are "too busy" or don't respond to situations that don't involve actual crimes in progress. Part of their function is to preserve the peace, stop crime before it happens, and serve your needs. It's easy to get frustrated sometimes when the law enforcement response is not as rapid or as thorough as you might like. If you think the delay in their response is unreasonably long, call the 9-1-1 dispatcher again and ask for an updated arrival time. If the situation was not handled to your satisfaction, call the station in your area and ask to speak to a police or sheriff's supervisor.

Employee Responsibilities:

<u>Home Visits for Medical, Maintenance, or Inspections:</u>

Don't go into unfamiliar buildings, homes, apartment units, or storage areas without first assessing the overall situation. Is it daylight, during working hours, or night and after-hours? Who is supposed to be in the building, home, or unit? Who is actually in the unit? Are there more people inside then you feel comfortable with?

You have the discretion to disengage and not complete your work if you believe your safety is in jeopardy. (Don't misuse this right; not every situation will call for you to leave without finishing your work.)

The presence of obvious weapons, gang insignias or graffiti on the walls of an apartment unit, narcotics or contraband inside a home should tell you it's not safe to go inside or stay there once you do go in. Assess the unit before you go inside as well as once you're inside.

If you need to find a creative way to get out of the unit, tell the people in the house or unit, "I just got an emergency call. I'll be right back after I go and take care of it." Leave the unit and call your supervisor when it's safe to do so.

Change the ratios of confrontation any time you feel threatened by the behavior, actions, or words of one or more people. Get help from co-workers or your supervisor to go along with you for problematic houses, businesses, or apartments.

Supervisor Responsibilities – Facility Safety:

For all facility mailrooms, get and post a copy of the US Postal Service's Poster #84 – "Handling Dangerous Mail." Remind all mail-handling employees to use latex gloves when handling the mail and report any delivered items (USPS, FedEx, UPS, etc.) that may contain hazardous, dangerous, or threatening messages involving real or implied threats to senior leaders, employees, premises, or facilities to management immediately. This should include any threatening correspondence to an employee or senior leader (from a disgruntled person, domestic violence partner, or stranger seeking to disrupt the business). Collect and protect all evidence and hold it for review by the police, as necessary.

Follow good mail handling and evacuation procedures in the event any employees come into contact with a dangerous mailed item, i.e., don't let them carry it around the facility. Seal off the area, isolate the employee(s), and call for emergency help.

Depending on your type of business, if you have group events, involving a large number (say 25 or more) of visitors, customers, vendors, clients, or taxpayers attending a meeting, conference, party, it may be necessary to create a Facility Safety Plan. This document should be created using a team approach, specifically with your safety and security stakeholders, focusing on getting people safely into and out of the facility in normal circumstances and during the rare possibility of an emergency.

It should cover the date; start and stop times; locations; a description of the event; an estimated attendance; contact information for the event leaders or sponsors; a schedule of activities during the event; how people will communicate normally or in an emergency (radios, cell phones, landline phones, Intranet, in-house messaging, texting); weather concerns, if any; evacuation points, interior or exterior assembly areas, or shelter in place gathering points; the need for uniformed or plainclothes security; police presence; medical concerns (hiring paramedics); parking controls; access control and any special badging for visitors, vendors, dignitaries, or employees; or any known threats to the attendees.

Trust your employees' feelings about unsafe environments or intimidating people. Just because it doesn't scare you, doesn't mean that it's not frightening to them. Realize they may not be able to tell you exactly why they don't want to go into someone's home. Sometimes it's hard to describe gut feelings. If it feels wrong for them, respect that and help them find a safe solution for the work they need to do.

Encourage your people to make good security decisions first and then explain their reasons second. Plenty of people who suppressed their intuitive feelings about a security situation had regrets later.

Employee Responsibilities:

Lost Child Situations:

For a child who appears lost, try to determine if the child knows his/her parent's names, address, cell phone numbers, or the names and numbers of other family members.

Find a translator, if necessary.

Provide supportive, verbal comfort to the child.

Do not move the child into the facility if you are alone.

If the child says he or she is a runaway who wants help, call the non-emergency number for law enforcement and make a report.

Don't turn the child over to anyone purporting to be a family member without verifying this first, including checking their ID, and making calls to confirm who he or she is and if this person has permission from the parent or guardian to pick up the child.

If it appears the child does not want to go with the family member or designated person, call 9-1-1 immediately and have law enforcement respond to verify the situation.

Found or Abandoned Property, Safety Concerns:

For those issues or incidents not involving crimes in progress, i.e., found narcotics; stripped, abandoned, or obvious stolen cars; or similar types of contraband, know that it may take a law enforcement representative hours (or even a day or more) to respond.

Protect any found property or evidence until law enforcement arrives.

For active safety issues (water leaks, road hazards, bee swarms, etc.), keep people out of the area as best as you can and get immediate help.

Tell your supervisor as much detail as you can and don't get caught up in the problem as you try to find a solution (get soaked, stung, or fall in a sinkhole, etc.).

Supervisor Responsibilities:

Don't let the situation get out of hand. If you can't solve it by using your good judgment first, get help. Many departments in your city or county can assist with most of the issues described in the examples.

Know who to call before you ever have to call. The first time to look for the exterminator vendor's number is not when the bees are swarming around your building.

Keep the number of employees involved in any situation down to a minimum. Gossip, unintended statements, and hovering around can make emotional or frightening situations worse.

Provide some information to calm people in the area, but don't admit liability or fault if it's related to your organization.

Know the location of your facility first-aid kits and decide if you need to bring them to a scene outside.

Don't touch or allow employees to touch any found

property or items that could be dangerous: firearms, syringes, narcotics, weapons, bloodstains, electrical lines, etc.

Get the names and unit numbers of all first responders and take pictures if possible. Write an incident report as soon as it's safe to do so.

Reporting Procedures:

It can help to have an "ICE Box" (a large In Case of Emergency plastic box, filled with a first aid kit, a master phone list, facility maps, extra keys or key cards) at all office locations. These boxes can be used inside the facility and can be brought outside for an incident near the building, especially if it involves an emergency evacuation.

FIRE, FIRST AID AND MEDICAL EMERGENCIES

Examples:

A building fire, a car fire in the parking lot, or a nearby wildfire. An employee having chest pains. A client, customer, or visitor who slips and falls on your property.

Important Information:

The good news is that if you work in a modern facility, chances are good it will have a state of the art fire alarm system, including ceiling sprinklers, smoke and temperature alarms, evacuation procedures, and maybe even a floor warden system. If you work in a historical building, you may not have all of these fire protection features, but overall, building fires in occupied offices, factories, and manufacturing plants are rare. You still need to pay attention and respond to fire alarms, smoke alarms, actual smoke or flames, fire drills, and evacuations.

You are not expected nor required to fight fires or provide medical aid as part of your job. However, safety is everyone's responsibility, especially our supervisors. In some more minor situations, you may be able to do enough to stop the problem on the spot. Examples include: helping an employee who has fainted, using a facility fire extinguisher on a small kitchen fire, or getting the facility first-aid kit and using the bandages to stop an employee's or visitor's minor wound.

Remember: When you call 9-1-1 from your cell phone, you may reach a state police dispatcher. You will need to tell them to transfer you to the Fire Department in your area.

Action Steps:

Employee Responsibilities:

Fire Emergency:

When it comes to any fire if you have even the smallest doubt about your ability to extinguish it, get yourself and everyone else out of the facility. It's not the flames that kill or incapacitate people; it's the smoke inhalation. Evacuate all employees and visitors, call 9-1-1 from a safe location and stay away from the building until you're told by uniformed fire personnel it's safe to enter.

Once all employees leave, they should never go back inside. Smoke kills more people than fire. You can always get another laptop, purse, or cell phone.

You should already know where the safety equipment

is for your facility. This includes fire extinguishers, flashlights, first-aid kits, smoke alarms, facility maps, and the fire alarm panels.

You should also know how to get out of any part of the building. Your usual escape routes posted on your emergency floor plans may be blocked by smoke, fire, or fallen debris. It's not important how you get out, just that you get out. Break a ground floor window if you have to. Meet at a pre-determined place far from the building where you can be medically assessed and counted.

Medical Emergency:

For medical emergencies, you should only do what you know how to do. For your own peace of mind and to help others and yourself, you should have a basic knowledge of first aid procedures, and know where the well-stocked, accessible first-aid kits are stored in your facility. You should take either a basic CPR class (where you learn to do chest compressions only on potential cardiac arrest victims); a more advanced CPR class (where you learn to give mouth to mouth resuscitation and chest compressions); AED training (if you have AEDs on-site); and even so-called "Stop the Bleed" training to know how and when to use tourniquets on yourself or others. (Go to www.bleedingcontrol.org for more information.)

But just as no law demands that you provide first aid to someone in need, you cannot be sued successfully for doing your best in a medical crisis (otherwise known as the "Good Samaritan Law"), unless you acted unreasonably, dangerously, or made the situation much worse. This should make it easier for you to take action to try and save someone's life.

As with a fire in or around the facility, know when to help, and when to help the first responders by clearing out of the area, offering the victims comfort, or providing the first responders with additional information, support, or use of the facility. Be ready to move people to an area inside or outside the building where they can be treated. Discuss with your colleagues how to use things like rolling chairs or blankets to help move injured employees.

When it comes to injuries that happen to employees at a facility, one habit all employees need to adopt is their continuing vigilance about what could be defined as "near-miss events." This means don't wait until there is a situation where someone has been hurt, say something to someone when you see something that could cause an injury. You can either send someone to get qualified help or post someone near enough to the hazardous situation while you go for help. In other words, don't leave a potentially bad situation unaddressed and hope someone else will report it. Examples include having a co-worker stand by a slippery spill why you go get some cleaning materials or standing by a faulty elevator door while a colleague goes to call a maintenance or facilities supervisor.

Supervisor Responsibilities:

Be ready to help evacuate all employees and visitors for any fire situation that appears to be spreading out of control.

Know your limits when it comes to fire or medical emergencies. Only do what you know or have been trained to do. It helps to know who has certain medical skills and certifications among your employees.

Remind all employees about the location of the safety equipment like first-aid kits, earthquake kits, blankets, chemical cleanup stations, etc.

Establish an annual walk-through process, where you take all employees in your department to the locations of the safety equipment and evacuation points. Consider this step as part of any new-employee orientation as well.

Remind all employees that for any situation requiring an evacuation, to get out of the facility any way they can. They should meet at a pre-determined staging location for building fires only, not for active shooter events.

For serious-injury situations, focus on the needs of your employees. After the situation and scene have stabilized, be a good professional witness and gather information for either the police or your organization's safety and security stakeholders to assist in their investigations. The first 24 hours are often the most critical information-gathering moments, especially if the incident has the potential for litigation. Both the plaintiffs and defense attorneys will want to know what you did, as a supervisor, before, during, and after the incident. As we know the lawyers like to say, "If you didn't write down what you did, it didn't happen."

Reporting Procedures:

If you're a manager or supervisor, know where to get and how to complete all forms or reports related to incidents and accidents that you have witnessed or been involved with.

If you're an employee, fully participate in the fact-finding and information-gathering portions of all incident reports. Tell the truth, tell what you saw or did, and support your organization's efforts to defend itself legally, accurately, and ethically.

FLU, ILLNESSES AND PANDEMICS

Examples:

The Coronavirus pandemic of 2020; the H1N1 virus from 2009; SARS; bird and swine flu; the Zika virus of 2016; and noroviruses, that cause stomach distress, as we've seen on large cruise ships.

Important Information:

From our government health agencies and medical providers, the best response to any virus outbreak seems to be hygiene and hibernation. Wash your hands for at least 20 seconds (sing Happy Birthday to yourself twice at the sink); avoid touching your face and mouth after you've touched other surfaces; contact your doctor and stay home if you develop flu-like symptoms like a fever, a cough, body aches, and shortness of breath.

You need to think about your health first, not just your career. We already know the US lags behind the rest of First World countries when it comes to employees taking vacation days. Workaholism was invented here. Some employees are afraid to take sick days, fearing they will be perceived as weak, not a good team player, or passed over for work assignments or promotions. This is not a reasonable approach, as it selfishly puts other employees or customers – some of whom may already have compromised immune systems – at risk of getting even sicker than you. Don't abuse your sick leave policies but don't store them up when you're actually sick.

Action Steps:

Employee Responsibilities:

Monitor your body for signs of sickness: unusual fatigue or muscle aches; a dry, unproductive cough that lingers or a wet cough that gets worse; fever for more than one day; rashes; stomach upset, nausea, or continued diarrhea; dizziness, or any other symptom that you know is not normal for your body. Is it a head cold, a sinus infection, allergies, or do you feel like you might have strep throat, bronchitis, or pneumonia? You don't always have to go to a medical doctor for every little ache or pain, but use good judgment and don't try to self-diagnose yourself using medical sites from the Internet. Most common colds and similar illnesses run their course in about a week, as long as you take a reasonable amount of appropriate medications, hydrate properly, and get more sleep.

Supervisor Responsibilities:

Don't create or allow a work culture where your employees are afraid to take sick days when they are actually sick, for fear of criticism, retaliation, missing out, or getting passed over. This only creates the kind of problems reasonable sick leave policies are supposed to prevent.

Business owners and operators must look at their sick day and employee longer-term leave policies with an eye toward more compassion, flexibility, and empathy.

If you're a manager or supervisor, you need to work with your Human Resources Department to clarify or adapt your sick leave policies: "If you're getting sick, stay home until you're medically ready to come back to work. We will accommodate your workload by making all necessary adjustments, without harm to your career. If you are able to work from home, we'll figure out a way for you to do that. We will be creative in our use of teleconferences, webinars, reorienting our priorities, and even extending paid sick time as necessary."

Pay attention to the national media for updated stories on possible pandemics and be ready to work with your safety and security team to follow their protocols for isolation, social distancing, or working from home.

Reporting Procedures:
During a possible pandemic, county public health agencies will collect and provide data from the communities they serve.

GANG PROBLEMS OR GANG VIOLENCE

Examples:

Back-and-forth gang graffiti between rival groups that escalates into a confrontation, fights, and then a series of retaliatory shootings. Gang members or gang "wannabes" loitering around our facilities. Gang members who threaten our employees face to face, anonymously, or through graffiti messages.

Important Information:

In many cities, gang membership numbers in the thousands. Law enforcement and social services agencies have long fought the battle to arrest, deter, or redirect street gang members. Today, we see children as young as eight and men in their 60s associated with street gangs. The problem crosses all races, all neighborhoods, all cities and communities, and even genders, with female gang members on the rise as well. These people are often armed, don't fear jail, prison, or being arrested, and don't have much sense of the value of human life, theirs or anyone else's.

The point is gang crime is a national, statewide, and local issue. There are no easy solutions; there is only our ability to work within the system we have. The police fight the gang battle every day, telling them, in effect, "You do not control this city. You do not own this neighborhood. This is our turf. You do not have the right to terrorize good people. You do not have the right to kill each other. We will never stop fighting against your violence."

We must all work as a security team, with each employee looking out for our co-workers, taxpayers, tenants, customers, and visitors. Use your intuition, tell others about your concerns when you fear gang activity is on the rise, and work with law enforcement to help them do what they need to do to battle this problem. When we are too afraid to stop gangs, they will always have power over us. It takes courage to stand up to these gangs. Working together, and with our community law enforcement and social services partners, is the right thing to do.

Action Steps:

Employee Responsibilities:

You may cross paths with gang members (or those who think they are or associate with known gang members) in your facilities and offices, in tenant housing, in the field, or in the streets and parking lots adjacent to our properties. In most situations, gang members will not cause or start confrontations with you for no reason. Often, their main concern is their safety from attack from other rival gangs. When alone, a gang member may act completely different from when this person is among his friends.

When in groups, however, their behavior may change to become more aggressive, hostile, sarcastic, or challenging. It's best not to confront them; simply ignore their comments and move on. To understand the gang, we have to focus on their most important currency: respect. Let's face it, gang members kill each other over the slightest moments of disrespect. When dealing with gang members in a business environment, be careful not to put them down, act superior, or speak or act in a condescending way. To say they are sensitive to insult is to understate their problem by half. Stay focused on whatever legitimate business transactions you have with them and help them get on their way.

In the field, if you come into contact with known gang members, and you have concerns for your safety while you work around them, speak with your boss (especially as a group of co-workers, seeking information, support, and protection together). In certain field situations, you may want or need to ask the local police or sheriff for assistance. There is much they can do using so-called "preserve the peace" calls to provide a "force presence" so you and your colleagues can do your work safely.

If you are ever threatened by one or more gang members, leave the area, and call the police immediately. Threats are a felony in most states and you have the right to make a report so law enforcement can investigate the incident and make arrests and/or demonstrate to the threateners that there are consequences to their words or actions. This includes any graffiti-based threats where you or other employees are mentioned by name. As scary as this situation appears, it will be worse if you don't report it to both law enforcement and your supervisor immediately. The police or sheriff can only help you if they know about the threat. Not reporting it gives the gang members the power to control you; this is not how you'll ever want to live, in constant fear.

Similarly, if you ever have any off-the-job conflicts with gang members, because of your work, you must report it to your supervisor or any other safety and security stakeholder immediately. Besides working with law enforcement, we may need to take certain steps to protect you at work.

It's not an issue of "bravery" or of handling your own business yourself; it's about protecting yourself, your family, your co- workers, and your organization from harm.

Supervisor Responsibilities:

Listen for street talk or any gossip about gang members or gang activity. Where there's smoke, there's usually fire. These types of criminals often foreshadow their next moves.

One of your primary tasks is to manage the fears that your employees have about their interactions with suspected or actual gang members. (You may have similar fears, which are reasonable considering the level of violence these people can attain.)

Use your law enforcement relationships, both on-site if you are at a location where you see the police on a regular basis, or through your use of 9-1-1 when the situation calls for police intervention. Stay in contact with your boss, Human Resources, Risk Management, and your Security Department (if applicable).

Encourage your employees to come to you with situations or negative contacts with gang members, so that you can help them come up with realistic solutions they can live with and work under.
Report any off-duty gang conflicts or negative contacts your employees may have to your police or sheriff's agency.

Reporting Procedures:

See if your city police or county sheriff has a Gang Unit. Find out what types of social service agency or grant-funded programs (often run by former gang members trying to give back non- violent solutions in their communities) you may be able to contact for help before a gang-related situation escalates.

HOMELESS PEOPLE AND TRESPASSERS

Examples:

A homeless man comes into your lobby or office, asking for money, looking for food, or asking to use the employee restroom. You encounter a homeless person on posted private property. You are threatened or harassed by a group of homeless people as you enter or leave your building.

Important Information:

We know that the societal problem of people experiencing homelessness is a serious social and political issue, but it's also a safety and security concern as well. Many chronically homeless people are seriously mentally ill and/or longtime substance abusers, who have great difficulty following the rules of the agencies who try to assist them. Most often, most people who are homeless fall into two categories: temporary or chronic. The majority of homeless individuals tend to be fairly docile, relatively cooperative when you tell them to leave, and not looking to cause a confrontation that would get them involved with the police and/or arrested. You can usually deal with them by being polite but firm: "You can't do that if you want to stay here" or "I'm not allowed to let you use our employee restroom" or "You can't bring your things into this building" or "I'm sorry, but you'll have to leave now."

A small part of the homeless population is predatory, violence-prone, and involved in thefts, assaults, robberies, or using violence against other homeless people, the public, or employees they encounter. For these aggressive, angry, violent types, you'll need to use space and distance, awareness, assertive communication skills, or even self-defense techniques to keep them away from you. Be prepared to call the police if any homeless individuals look like their drug or alcohol behavior or mental health problems cause them to become violent.

Trespassers, who may or not be homeless, may come on to our properties to look for a shortcut to where they are going; seek out other criminal associates or rival gang members; or look for opportunities to rob people, steal property or cars, sell narcotics, or vandalize things. Call law enforcement if you see trespassers who don't move out of the area or who appear ready to commit crimes.

For either of these groups of people, you don't always have to challenge them. If you decide to make contact, try to have one or more co-workers or a supervisor with you. If you are threatened, disengage, get to a safe place and call 9-1-1. Tell the dispatcher why the person's behavior concerns you. (Don't use labels like "he's crazy"; describe what this person is doing, what he or she looks like, and why you need a police response.)

Action Steps:

Employee Responsibilities:

People experiencing homelessness in and around our property can sometimes become a permanent fixture in or around the worksite. You'll likely see the same people regularly. You can use this to your advantage by setting the boundaries for their behavior early and often.

Try a lighter touch. Nobody likes to be told what to do in a mean way or lectured about policies, laws, or rules. You need to be firm, fair, reasonable, assertive, and consistent as you deal with anyone. Protecting this person's dignity, treating him or her as a human being, and even using a little humor can go a long way toward gaining his or her compliance.

Set boundaries by giving the person some choices: "If you want to stay here, you can, but you can't bother people," or "You can come in but you have to leave your stuff outside."

Use your intuition and decide to call 9-1-1 before it gets out of control. If you feel the situation is escalating, disengage, and get some help from a co-worker or a supervisor.

Try not to give homeless people money, clothing, or food every time you see them at your workplace. This will only encourage them to come around (along with their friends) and disrupt our business operations.

Don't allow them to use rear-area employee restrooms, go inside your facilities unescorted or unnoticed, or get past the lobby or reception doors.

If a situation escalates, remove yourself and your employees from the area and call 9-1-1. If he/she continues to argue or threaten you or others, tell the person to leave, disengage yourself, and call the police (or have a co-worker go and do it while you try to talk the person into leaving).

Trespassers:

Most real criminals don't like to be publicly observed. They prefer to work in stealth, darkness, or without notice. Being vigilant in and around your facilities continuously can deter many would-be criminals, especially if they believe that if you see them preparing to act, you will call the police and identify them later.

If you feel comfortable, based on your personality and communication skills, challenge people who don't look like they belong on our property: "Sir, can I help you? What office are you looking for or who are you trying to find? Are you visiting someone here? Do you have an appointment?" Don't let strangers into your facility without verifying their ID and their legitimate business reasons for being there.

Just because someone is wearing a work uniform doesn't mean you still shouldn't ask for his or her valid ID. If you don't recognize the usual delivery driver, repair or maintenance person, or vendor, don't let him or her just walk right past without checking in with you first.

Criminals usually always use surveillance of their target before they act. This includes behaviors we can see them do: looking into a car window, climbing over a fence into the back of a factory or Public Works yard, looking over their shoulders for witnesses or the police. If you see these behaviors and your intuitive feelings suggest to you it's not right, tell your supervisor, your co-workers, and call 9-1-1. Describe the person's behavior to the 911 Dispatcher: "He's carrying a screwdriver and trying to pry open car doors in our lot."

Supervisor Responsibilities:

Monitor all employee encounters with homeless people or potential or actual trespassers for signs of escalation or violence. Be ready to call 9-1-1.

If you feel comfortable dealing with homeless people (based on past contacts with them, your experiences with the same people over and over, etc.), have your employees accompany you to talk with them and adapt your style of managing their behavior.

Look for people "casing" your property. If their pre-attack behavior seems suspicious, either challenge their right to be on our property or call for law enforcement help immediately.

Develop contacts with local public and private resource agencies in your neighborhood that could assist the homeless population in and around your worksite.

Reporting Procedures:

It can help to recognize the differences between people who are loitering in and around the perimeter of your work area versus people who want to come inside and steal, threaten, or hurt people. The first group may have no place else to go, be bored, or have just wandered by. The second group has come to cause problems. The first group will usually comply if you ask them to leave. The second group may cause confrontations. Be ready with an approach for both groups.

INTERNAL THREATS, IT SECURITY AND ECONOMIC ESPIONAGE

Examples:

A co-worker steals company financial information and sells it to a competitor. A co-worker steals cash from the company, commits fraud or embezzlement, or steals company products and sells them online. An outsider hacks into your IT system and shuts it down, demanding a ransom to start it back up again. A colleague brings a competitor into the building after hours to take pictures of a new product. A co-worker posts personal information about employees on the Dark Web. Employees post company or agency proprietary data on their personal social media sites.

Important Information:

These examples may sound like they're either unlikely or are scenes out of a spy movie, but theft, fraud, embezzlement, hacking, and economic espionage are serious and expensive realities. Foreign competitors (including governments) actively look for ways to exploit untrustworthy employees of American companies to gain an economic advantage. The so-called "disgruntled employee," who hates his or her boss or co-workers and the organization, can offer a lot of excuses, rationalizations, and justifications as to why it's perfectly acceptable to steal money, goods, information, or trade secrets. Groups of cyber crooks attack the IT systems of public and private sector organizations, intending to disrupt the business or by stealing money or information.

Some employees unknowingly participate in these crimes by providing information to hackers who call in and use social engineering techniques to manipulate them, e.g., "Hi this is Dave from IT. We're doing a systems check on the server. Could you provide me with your log-in information so I can verify that your e-mail is working correctly?" Be wary of any attempts to get you to reveal personal, financial, or protected information to strangers, online, over the phone, and in person. Pay attention to the safety of your personal and company or agency property.

Action Steps:

Be instantly suspicious of any phone call you get from someone claiming to work for your organization who asks a lot of prying questions about anything related to passwords, e-mail accounts, financial or personnel data, or your IT system. Verify who you are talking to before you provide any information. You should know who is who in your IT Department and legitimate employees should identify themselves correctly.

Follow a "clean desk, clean screen policy" each night

when you leave work. Make certain all your important papers or hard copy file folders are stored in your locked desk. Log off your computer so that no one can get access to any of your screen information or files or the Intranet or Internet. It's easy to get into the habit of skipping these steps because nothing bad has ever happened before and what's the likelihood of something bad happening now? Take the time to sanitize the hard copy and electronic data in your work area before you leave for home. (It's not unusual for cleaning crews to use your Internet systems after hours.)

When in doubt, either don't print it or shred it instead of throwing it away. The contents of your trash can should reveal nothing critical about your work, your organization, or you. Make sure you collect your copies from the copy machine as well.

Employee Responsibilities:

No one expects you to spy on your colleagues, but it's important to pay attention to what you see and hear, both in the workplace and online. You may stumble on to a paper trail, see a series of meetings between a colleague and an obvious outsider, discover odd online activities, or see products going out the door in a way that can't be accounted for. If it sounds strange or seems unusual, it probably is.

When it comes to illegal or unethical behaviors, you need to have the courage to tell one of your safety and security stakeholders. Notify the HR Director, your boss, Security (if you have that function), a department director or business leader, or your IT Director, if you suspect any illegal activity is going on.

Your organization may have an ethics hotline or an Ombudsman's Office where you can make an anonymous report if you are fearful of retaliation.

Supervisor Responsibilities:

Work with your leadership team to develop systems, policies, and protocols to combat fraud, theft, embezzlement, inventory theft, and the manipulation of your critical company data. Monitor your employees' work activities and interactions – not in a micromanaging way but what we might call "benevolent oversight" to make sure things are functioning as they should and people are doing what they are supposed to do.

Pay attention to inventory control issues and watch for the theft of not only expensive warehouse assets but also tools, parts, machinery, PCs, laptops, tablets, high-dollar office supplies (like printer ink or laser printer toner). You have the obligation to watch for secretive, manipulative, or potentially dishonest behaviors, in- person and online, and report what you know.

Monitor the employee work culture for fear, bullying, resentment, or "disgruntlement." Lots of aggrieved or dissatisfied employees feel justified in stealing from their organizations based on how they feel they have been treated by their bosses. Talk with your peers, Department Director, IT, HR, and Security if you have concerns. Happy employees are much less likely to commit fraud, theft, and economic espionage. Unhappy employees will rationalize these behaviors as a way to "payback" the organization for their perceived mistreatment.

Reporting Procedures:

As an employee, you don't have to confront your co-workers or "investigate them." Your role is to report unethical or suspicious behavior to your safety and security stakeholders so they can follow-up and follow-through.

PANIC BUTTONS

Examples:

Panic alarms or panic buttons that are installed under public counters or under reception desks. These hidden buttons may ring to a manager or supervisor's office, to a security officer's desk in the facility, to an alarm company, who will notify the police, or straight to the police department. Based on the type of people they encounter or the work they do, some employees may wear personal panic alarms on their belts or on breakaway lanyards around their necks.

Important Information:

The nature of your engagement with certain customers, clients, taxpayers, visitors, vendors, and others who enter your building, seek information, have complaints, or are upset over some issue, means that we need to have a way for our front counter or public- contact employees to notify our safety and security stakeholders in the event of a conflict or confrontation that escalates to a life- threatening situation. The use of panic buttons, typically installed underneath the public-contact counters, gives employees the ability to safely and covertly press a silent alarm, which will notify your leadership team, and/or the on-duty Lobby Security Officer, and if necessary, the police or sheriff's department dispatchers, who will send officers or deputies to the scene.

Your safety and security stakeholders will be responsible for the implementation and administration of this policy, to ensure the safety of all employees. Your leadership team may work in consultation with local law enforcement for additional guidance on the best use of panic buttons and panic alarms. It's important to establish a safety and security protocol for the responsible and effective use of panic alarms and panic buttons installed in our facilities, to prevent their misuse, accidental deployments, or miscommunication, especially during a real emergency.

Action Steps:

Employee's Responsibilities:

All employees are authorized to use a panic button or panic alarm in any encounter with a person entering our buildings who has threatened harm to them or others.

This includes any people:

- engaged in an Active Shooter or Armed Attacker event;

- making workplace violence threats (e.g., the person threatens to return to our facilities with a gun);

- making bomb or terroristic threats in person;

- intentionally displaying firearms, knives, or any other obvious weapons;

- making domestic violence threats to harm an employee;

- displaying violent mentally ill behaviors that make themselves a danger to self or others;

- making any threat of physical harm to employees or others, either over the counter or in the field.

(Panic buttons are not to be used for persons making threats to harm over the telephone. Report these situations to your supervisor, who will make the decision to contact the police.)

Employees should make the personal or group decision to press the panic button or panic alarm if they would call 9-1-1 in a similar situation elsewhere in their personal lives. As an adult employee working in a professional environment, you don't need permission from a supervisor to press a panic alarm, if your intuition tells you that's the right thing to do to keep yourself, other employees, and customers, visitors, or taxpayers safe from threats or violence from another person. Be ready to explain why you pressed the panic button once the situation has stabilized and become safe. We want to learn from every event, so we can improve our responses, protocols, training, and policies.

The panic button system is primarily designed for employees who work at front counters not protected by full-height bulletproof or shatter-resistant safety glass. For employees who work at fully- contained counters where it is unlikely the threatening person can harm them, they need to make a judgment call to either use the panic button, disengage from the person on the other side of the glass and call 9-1-1 from a safe location, or send another co- worker to go call 9-1-1 from a place of safety.

Employees should do their best to press a panic button or a panic alarm in a way that is not obvious to the threatening person. This can give our leadership team and the police time to respond, to observe the person's behavior, and decide as to what to do before the person leaves the scene. If the danger of the situation escalates after pressing the panic button, all employees need to leave the area as quickly and safely as possible, taking other taxpayers, visitors, or others with them, if possible, to a safe location.

Note: Certain crisis medical events, like a sudden heart attack or a severe bleeding injury, could benefit from using the panic button or panic alarm if the witnessing employee cannot get to a landline or cell phone to call for emergency medical care.

Supervisor's Responsibilities:

Upon hearing the panic button/panic alarm notification, the supervisor in charge of that department who is physically present in that location may:

- move to the nearest security camera monitor that shows the area where an employee used the panic button and make a rapid assessment of the situation before going to the counter to provide assistance;

- talk to nearby employees while moving to the counter area, to get information or an update as to the seriousness of the situation;

- call 9-1-1 and describe why the police need to send officers. Supervisors should use a landline telephone inside the building as his or her first choice, because this will ring directly to the police dispatchers. Supervisors should only use their cell phones if it is not safe to use a landline phone. Cell calls may be answered by the State Police, so there could be a delay to get transferred to the nearest local dispatch center.

Reporting Procedures:

In the event an employee pushes the panic button at his or her location for a real event (not an accidental use), the appropriate department supervisor for that location will provide a written report as to the nature of the incident, the response, and what actions were taken to the Department Director, the Human Resources Department, and the Facilities Department for a review of the incident and the use of the panic button. Actions taken could include a supervisor handling the situation without the need for a police response, a police response resulting in a detention for a mental health evaluation, or an arrest for a criminal violation.

Supervisors will also fully report all situations where the panic button use resulted in an injury or ambulance response for any employee or citizen involved in the event.

In the event there are repeated accidental presses of the panic button or employees are using the button for non-emergency or low-threat situations, your leadership team will review these incidents to either relocate or reposition the buttons or provide additional safety and security awareness training to the employees in question.

The panic buttons will be checked (monthly or quarterly) to ensure they work properly, are reporting the correct location, and need to be recorded on a Panic Alarm Log.

ROBBERY PREVENTION

Examples:

An armed or unarmed robber enters a retail store, pharmacy, bank, or office with the intent to steal cash or other goods by using force, a weapon, or fear. Some are armed with guns or knives, others may simulate that they have a weapon. Some robbers specialize in robberies at ATMs, parking garages or parking lots, or any place there are people with money, cash registers, or things that can be stolen, spent, sold, or pawned.

Important Information:

Robbers are highly erratic people. We can never accurately predict or completely prevent crime or violence, no matter what we do.

We can deny, deter, and delay people who seek to rob our stores, facilities, or businesses. We must use good security devices, intelligent policies and procedures, and a strong relationship with law enforcement.

It's not easy, wise, or safe to make generalizations about robbers and their potential behaviors. Some are quite fearful and anxious during the event and will run away if their original plans fail.

Others are quite violent and enjoy the process of terrorizing or hurting people. Some always carry weapons, others never do.

Almost all robbers will visit the place they want to rob before they attempt this crime. Many robbers case the store two to four hours before, on the day of the incident, often wearing the same clothing, minus their hats or masks. Casers usually come in on the same day, to make sure nothing has changed from the last time they cased it. Don't be afraid to look directly at casers who come inside the store or sit in their cars. Let them know they have been seen.

Some robbers work with a partner who is not seen by others unless he needs to protect the other robber from interference or alert him as to the arrival of the police.

The motive for nearly all robberies is to support a drug habit, a gambling habit, or both. A small number of robberies are done by the mentally ill, or new or wannabe gang members, usually in the company of a hardcore gang member.

The more robberies the suspect has done in the past, the braver he may feel. This can be good or bad, since he may be less frightened and therefore more aggressive, or more in control and less likely to screw it up and shoot someone.

Most robbers want quick cash, freeway closeness, and exits near freeways; they don't want to drive aimlessly or rapidly through unfamiliar streets.

Action Steps:

Employee Responsibilities:

The most common advice for your involvement in an armed or simulated armed robbery is to give over the money or items the robber wants. Giving up the money is the best course of action and not resisting is all about protecting yourself, your customers, and your co-workers.

When alone with a person in the store who makes you feel uncomfortable, use a "phantom employee callout" to make it seem like more than one employee is on duty. Call out to the back room and say, "I'll take care of this customer, Dave. Finish stocking the cooler." You're trying to make the robber have doubts as to how many people are in the store.

Watch for "distraction teams" – a screaming woman, a crying baby, or an injured person. Keep your eyes on the register.

Keep the store and register keys separate from your personal house or car keys.

Don't carry your wallet while working or keep your purse nearby.

Be extra vigilant during opening or closing times, employee shift changes, and police shift changes.

During an actual robbery:

- Make no sudden moves. Talk quietly and don't ask questions.

- Open the register and step back from the counter slowly. Consider turning sideways from the robber to present less of a full target.

- Keep your hands at waist-level, not raised up or hidden. Don't stare or argue.

- Always believe there are at least two robbers.

- Try to slow down your breathing and stay out of "fight or flight" mode.

- When it's safe to do so, lock the main doors and call the police first (call your manager, family, or others later) from your facility phone. Be a good witness and wait for the police from a place of safety. Tell the dispatcher who you are, where you are, and what just happened.

- The dispatcher and responding police will want to know this information about the robber and any accomplices:

Race / Sex / Age / Clothing / Weapons?
Time of crime Number of suspects
Car – color, year, make, model, body style, dents, stickers, tinted windows
Direction of travel on foot or by car Height / Weight
Hair / Eyes / Build
Unique traits – tattoos, scars, etc.

Protect the scene and any evidence.

Have courage and help the criminal justice system to catch and prosecute these criminals.

Supervisor Responsibilities:

If you manage a public front counter that dispenses money or accepts payments, you have to consider the possibility your staff can get robbed.

One robber at the desk or counter might mean one or more inside or outside too. Check for this on your security cameras.

Train your employees to lock the doors, call 9-1-1 first, (not the manager, a family member, or a loved one), and speak to the police immediately as soon as it is safe.

Create a pre-printed checklist for employees to write down the description of the suspect after he or she has fled.

Don't reveal too much about your security equipment or procedures used at your facility. All information must be on a "need to know" basis.

Develop special procedures for when employees working alone have to leave the floor or for restroom breaks.

Remove all posters from the windows, apply tint, create full line of sight, keep the rear doors locked, and maintain all interior and exterior lighting fixtures.

Put more barriers in the business to make it hard for the crooks to get in and out quickly (displays, aisles, counters, turnstiles, double doors).

Install fences or gates to block off the rear of the store (a favorite pre-robbery hiding place or post-robbery escape route).

Install speed bumps and concrete planter boxes in the parking lot to make it tougher on the getaway driver. Install high-quality pixel image (not analog) cameras and a large TV monitor / flat screen at the main entrance to your facility and let everyone see themselves big and bold, as they enter.

Make the investment in network storage, upgraded hard drives, and updated software for your camera systems. They will pay for themselves over time.

Encourage your employees to pay closer attention to potential robbers. Casers come in a few hours before the robbery, most often on the same day, to make sure nothing has changed from the last time. Have your employees make eye contact and say hello to everyone they encounter.

Keep the back and side door entrances of your facility locked at all times.

In office environments, keep lines of sight clear and unblocked to the lobby and customer areas (not covered by plants, file cabinets, dividers, etc.).

Teach your employees to have "Sundown Vigilance" and increase their security awareness around the end of the business day.

Take better physical care of your money. Be more security- conscious while moving it or handling it in bulk. If you have to help the employee with cash management, close the register temporarily and do it discreetly, without any customers seeing it.

Change the daily routine for depositing the cash. Move portable safes to new locations. Change the combinations for safes and vaults on an irregular basis. Use different people, times, cars, methods, bags, and routes to the bank. Better yet, hire an armored car service; it's cheap insurance.

Security guards are not a good replacement for cameras; they're mutually exclusive.

Make sure the camera system you choose is installed correctly. The view(s) must be visible at night and in bright sunlight. Test the TV or computer screen images regularly.

Make the investment in a camera system you can access from your laptop or from home.

Use a digital camera system where the images are stored in the cloud or on a hard drive. These can be copied to a DVD later for the police. Block camera blind spots with furniture or displays.

Never install fake cameras. Having a camera system that does not record or displays only to a TV screen is useless and may subject you to liability from people who get injured, expecting that someone was watching the event unfold, and was supposed to call the police.

Change the position of the security guards frequently. Sometimes their visual presence is useful; other times they should watch from a position of stealth.

The first hour is critical for police patrol officers to make an arrest; the first 24 hours are critical for detectives to make an arrest.

Provide good descriptions of people and cars first; provide good photos and videos later.

Some robberies are known as "inside jobs." This is often the result of an employee committing the crime, or more likely, telling his or her friends, or friends of friends, about how much money is kept in a cash register inside the business. Do your best to discourage your employees from talking to anyone about money or security procedures.

Some robbers are good social engineers and may talk to employees about security procedures or devices in seemingly casual conversations. The police will want to know who knew about the important details concerning amounts of cash, cash handling, and security devices or procedures.

Reporting Procedures:

Call the police if you see one or more people look like they are casing the areas in or around your facility. Be ready to give full and accurate descriptions to the dispatcher.

It's important to call the police as soon as it's safe to do so. They need your information to catch the robbers before they get too far away.

SELF-DEFENSE AT WORK

Examples:

Protecting yourself from assaults by current or former co-workers, irate visitors, vendors, customers, taxpayers, ratepayers, strangers, either face-to-face, over the phone, or in the field.
Staying safe in field encounters, while making home visits, and during high-risk encounters. Keeping vigilant to protect yourself from robberies, sexual assaults, or parking lot attacks.

Important Information:

You have the right to defend yourself from being assaulted by anyone in your workplace or out in the field, working on behalf of your organization. If you have a field job where you work in uniform and have contact with irate, uncooperative, or threatening taxpayers, you may have several choices to help protect yourself, including: OC Pepper Spray; personal audible alarms; ASP-type expandable batons; tactical knives and flashlights; Tasers; or even a firearm. (Make certain you have been given permission, have been trained, and are certified for any weapons you carry on behalf of your employer. Give copies of your training certificates to your boss or HR.)

If you don't work in those types of jobs, your options are probably limited to OC Pepper Spray, an audible alarm, and a tactical flashlight.

Guns in the workplace is a complex legal, moral, and ethical issue. There is much national debate about establishing "gun-free zones" versus allowing employees to protect themselves from a mass attacker. Most company or agency policies strictly prohibit their employees from carrying or storing firearms in their building, even if they have a Concealed Carry permit or their particular state allows for concealed carry without a permit. Some organizations allow their employees to store firearms in their personal cars while parked on company or agency property; others prohibit this as well. Know what you need to know to stay in compliance with the laws or policies for your particular state, county, and organization.

Action Steps:

If you decide to carry OC Pepper Spray, actually carry it in your hand as you leave your building and head to your car, the bus stop, the train station, etc. No need to wave it around, since you should be able to carry it discreetly, but do carry it. Put it away only when your intuition tells you it's safe to do so. Too many people carry it in their purse, backpack, briefcase, or pocket, where it's not easy to get to in the stress of an attack.

Buy the OC Pepper Spray canister with the highest

concentration percentage of Oleoresin Capsicum that you can find. Most OC canisters range from 0.8 percent to three percent in strength. Law enforcement officers carry OC that is closer to two percent. The more the better, since in lower concentrations, it may not work as effectively on people who are psychotically mentally ill, under the influence of drugs or alcohol, or highly determined not to be stopped.

Once you buy your canister, take it outside on a non-windy day and test the spraying distance. Wipe a small amount under your eye so you can note its effects. The bad news is it burns on your skin and makes your eyes tear and sting. The good news is that you can still run away, protect yourself, or fight back even if some of your spray gets in your eyes or on your face. It won't kill you or stop you from breathing. Wash it off with a dilution of baby shampoo and cool water.

There are five steps you need to remember when it comes to using OC Pepper Spray:

1. Carry it in your hand.
2. Shake it before you use it on someone, to mix the chemicals.
3. Warn the person he or she will be sprayed if he or she tries to attack you. (Do this only if you have the time and distance to do it safely. Don't let the person come too close to you or try to disarm you.)
4. Spray the attacker's face and eyes until he or she stops attacking.
5. Leave the area quickly and call the police from a safe place.
6.

Employee Responsibilities:

You're responsible for carrying, storing, or protecting any self- defense weapons you are issued or allowed to possess while working. Use a locked desk or a lockable storage area (and don't store any weapons in your personal or company/agency car).

You must be "reasonable" in your use of force when it comes to protecting yourself against anyone who wants to harm you. This is a court-tested phrase that says you can't use more force than a reasonable person would use to stop an attack. That means you can only use self-defense techniques and physical force necessary to stop the threat and safely escape.

Supervisor Responsibilities:

Monitor any Security Incident Reports for threats or assaults between or against your employees. Encourage them to tell you or other supervisors about incidents where they have felt fearful, threatened, or bullied by anyone they encounter as part of their work, including current or former employees; their current or former spouses; customers, clients, taxpayers, ratepayers, visitors, vendors; strangers or aggressive homeless people; or criminals. Be ready to work with them and your security or law enforcement professionals to respond, address current or future safety or security issues, and solve these problems.

Reinforce and remind all employees about any weapons policies you may have. In some organizations, employees with certain jobs may be able to ask for and get permission to carry various weapons to keep themselves safe. As a boss, you may be able to start that discussion with your senior leadership to make those policy changes happen and better protect your staff.

Reporting Procedures:

If you are ever forced to protect yourself or use a self-defense weapon against someone who has threatened or attacked you, call the police and make a report once you are safe. If the police respond and can detain the suspect, be willing to make a citizen's arrest. You don't have to handcuff the person, just say you want the person arrested and sign the complaint form for the officer or deputy.

This is important to do for several reasons. For a misdemeanor not committed in the officer's presence (they didn't see it directly happen), they can't make an arrest. They can only warn the person and let him or her go. (They still may be able to arrest him or her for warrants, or being under the influence or in possession of drugs or weapons.) Second, you want the person who tried to harm you to face consequences in the criminal justice system. No consequences for his or her behavior and we all know it will continue. Third, you should not be fearful of retaliation from the attacker if you have him or her arrested.

Those cases are rare and usually involve gang members. Ask the reporting officer or deputy to use your work contact information, not your home or personal contact information.

TERRORISM AWARENESS

Examples:

There are three men parked in a van, which has been in the same spot for at least four hours. They seem to be taking photographs of the outside of your factory. An unknown person calls your office, saying he works for your burglar alarm company and he wants to verify your alarm codes with you. The security officer that works the graveyard shift in our facility reports that the same car has driven through the empty employee parking lot at different times, over the past two weeks.

Each of these scenarios may be completely harmless and connected to a valid explanation. However, these people may be targeting our buildings or our employees.

Important Information:

It's no surprise that we learn many life lessons in the aftermath of difficult or tragic events. Many people install burglar alarms in their homes only after a burglary or put in a car alarm only after their car is stolen. Therefore, our focus on terrorism, airport security, facility evacuation plans, and personal safety only began in earnest after the 9-11 tragedies. Here is some of what we have learned since that day:

Real bombers don't make bomb threats.

As we've discussed previously, fake bomb threats are most often called into public or private-sector companies by disgruntled current or former employees, mentally ill people, taxpayers or customers wanting revenge, or juveniles. Consider the actions of the Boston Marathon bombers, Ted Kaczynski (the Unabomber), Timothy McVeigh (Oklahoma City), and the bombers in the first World Trade Center attack in 1993. None of their murderous activities were preceded by warnings, calls, e-mails, or notes.

Unlike other countries, where planted bombs are occasionally revealed before they can detonate, this is not what happens in the United States. Real bombers make bombs and not bomb threats. Bomb threat makers make bomb threats and not real bombs.

Get out of the building any way you can.

Our review of mass evacuations has shown us that too often the best-created plans for a calm, orderly, and complete building evacuation will not work under the stress of the moment. As you review your facility evacuation plan, know that the entrance nearest you may be blocked by fire, debris, bad people, other scared employees, or other hazards. It's not where you get out, but how you get out that's most important. If this means you'll have to break a ground floor window to climb out or use a back stairs exit, then do that. You should already know every escape alternative.

Don't stage in one meeting spot.

Just like the evacuation route that no longer works, you may have to find an alternative place to meet following a building evacuation. While it's important to gather at a pre-determined location to be counted for a fire event, it's smart not to stage together during a bomb threat or workplace violence shooting.

Evacuate in many directions and return only when you know it's safe to do so.

Don't jam cell phone lines during a serious emergency.

While it can be hard to suppress the urge to call family and friends during a serious event, remember that everyone else has the same idea. Too many cell calls to 9-1-1 can overwhelm the local network system, so no one, including the first responders, can phone in or out. Know that if it's big, your police and fire protection agencies will surely know about it. Call out only when the situation has stabilized, limit the number of your calls, and keep them as brief as possible.

One of the most significant challenges our nation faced during the events like 9-11 or the 2020 pandemic was how to keep working when we really want to be home, with our loved ones, or just waiting at work for more national media updates.

Understandably, it's nearly impossible to focus on working when you're worried about off-the-job safety concerns like a terror attack in our country. Know that in the event of a significant terror attack, the senior leadership will make hard decisions as to how or if to continue to staff our facilities. Some employees may have to stay and others may be allowed to leave. While we realize you have personal concerns, you should make every reasonable effort to continue to do your job well, under the stress of the moment.

Here are some considerations for pre and post-terrorism responses for you to consider for your home:

- Pay attention to unusual sights, sounds, people, or groups in your neighborhood and community.

- Have emergency supplies at home, especially water, gas, cell chargers, toiletries, food, flashlights and their batteries, and cash.

- Create several meeting places near your house, in your neighborhood, or in your community if your family can't get back home.

- Monitor the media, but don't always believe the first stories. Wait for updates before you make decisions.

- In the event of a mass terror attack on your city, expect to have to live without lights, water, or electronic devices (gasoline pumps, ATMs, TVs, water pumps, stoves and ovens, freezers, refrigerators, etc.) for days. Have a plan in place to either hunker down with your stored emergency supplies or leave your home with your loved ones and pets until your community systems are re-established.

Action Steps:

In terms of keeping yourself safe from harm while at work, commuting to work, or out in your community, there are three ways to live your life:

Condition White – Unaware, not paying attention, caught by total surprise when bad things happen.

Condition Yellow – Aware, focused on the people and situations going on around you. Paying attention, using your intuition, and being ready to respond to an attack or an event with confidence.

Condition Red – Taking direct and immediate action to protect yourself or others, as necessary. Relying on your intuition, training, life experience, self-defense choices, tools, supplies, and equipment, and your pre-planned ability to make smart choices under pressure.

It's not possible to stay in Condition Red forever; it's just too stressful and demanding. You can and should, however, stay in Condition Yellow during those times when you're at work, dealing with the public, or out in the community.

Who is in charge of safety & security at our facilities? Every director, manager, supervisor. Every employee, full or part-time. Even our clients, customers, taxpayers, ratepayers, tenants, and vendors can tell us about situations we need to address.

It's up to us to take care of each other. We can't ignore or defer safety and security problems as "someone else's job." Through their interactions with other outside people (customers, clients, taxpayers, vendors, visitors, strangers) in the office or in the field, our employees can see and hear things that relate to keeping us all safe and protected.

Often, you will know about a security concern (for example, people watching our buildings or taking pictures) long before your local police or sheriff discovers it.

Report what you see to your safety and security stakeholders. Together, we can keep each other safe and make a difference in our workplaces and communities.

Employee Responsibilities:

As with any possible crime and security problem, if you believe you see suspicious indicators – people or situations that don't look, sound, or feel right – don't wait until it's too late to tell your co-workers or boss or call your local law enforcement agency. One of the primary functions of police officers and sheriff's deputies is to preserve the peace and investigate situations that could lead to crimes or violence before they happen. Do your part to keep your community and our nation safe. You could save countless lives with just one phone call. Don't let others talk you out of your intuitive feelings. Ask, "What would a reasonable person do?", then take appropriate actions based on your hunches, feelings, and observations.

Develop "vigilance behavior." Politely challenge people you don't know who aren't wearing visible identification inside your facility. Don't just assume that unknown people wearing work shirts or work uniforms are who they say they are. Make them prove it through their valid ID before you let them have complete access to any part of your facilities.

Know your part in the emergency procedures for your facility. If your facility conducts evacuation, fire, medical, active shooter, or similar response drills, practice them as if the event was real.

Supervisor Responsibilities:

Listen to your employees if they speak to you about people or situations that seem odd, fear-creating, or linked to current news stories, law enforcement warnings, safety or security bulletins, or other seemingly unrelated data, that in fact, may be part of a bigger picture. Terrorists don't often look like terrorists; they attempt to blend with their surroundings and they often fail because of vigilance from people who actually live or work in the area they are preparing to attack.

The Violence Equation for terrorism is:

Motive + Opportunity = Threat Potential

We will not always know the motive of a terrorist, nor can we usually ever change it. We can only seek to disrupt their opportunities by challenging our fears and remaining watchful.

Every terrorism attack is always preceded by surveillance. Bad people are deterred by good security policies, procedures, and devices, constant awareness, sharing information with others, and reporting suspicious indicators.

"Suspicious indicators" include:

- People watching our buildings.
- Cars parked nearby for too long.
- People driving by, taking notes or measurements, videotaping, or asking questions about us.
- Mail or packages we're not expecting.
- People dressed as vendors who are not known to us.
- Anything that's out of the ordinary or not normal for our parking lots, streets, or facilities.

Any of these should cause you to look further or report it. You don't have to confront bad people doing or getting ready to do bad things. Be ready to call the police to have them contact potential bad people and have them verify your concerns.

Reporting Procedures:

Besides your local law enforcement agencies, you can also contact your nearest FBI office, which includes the FBI Joint Terrorism Task Force or JTTF. Here's some information about the FBI Joint Terrorism Task Force (from the www.FBI.gov website):

"The FBI's Joint Terrorism Task Forces, or JTTFs, are our nation's front line of defense against terrorism, both international and domestic. They are groups of highly trained, locally based, passionately committed investigators, analysts, linguists, and other specialists from dozens of U.S. law enforcement and intelligence agencies. When it comes to investigating terrorism, they do it all: chase down leads, gather evidence, make arrests, provide security for special events, collect and share intelligence, and respond to threats and incidents at a moment's notice.

"JTTFs serve as a national resource and create familiarity among investigators and managers before a crisis by conducting frequent training to maintain the specialized skills of investigators, analysts, and crisis response teams. JTTFs pool talents, skills, and knowledge from across the law enforcement and intelligence communities into a single team that responds together.

The task forces coordinate their efforts largely through the interagency National Joint Terrorism Task Force, working out of FBI Headquarters, which makes sure that information and intelligence flow freely among the local JTTFs and beyond.

The first JTTF was established in New York City in 1980. Today there are about 200 task forces around the country, including at least one in each of the FBI's 56 field offices, with hundreds of participating state, local, and federal agencies.

JTTFs are working around the clock to protect you, your families, and your communities from terrorist attacks."

VANDALISM, TAGGING AND GRAFFITI

Examples:

Gang or "tagger crew" graffiti painted on our buildings, windows, doors, or vehicles. Damage caused by etching marks or physical force (broken door or gate locks, light fixtures, windows, etc.).

Vandalism to company or agency property or an employee's personal property. Threats to or from other gangs, gang members, tenants, or employees communicated via graffiti messages.

Important Information:

Graffiti and vandalism caused by gang members, taggers, and teenagers are significant, expensive, on-going problems for many cities and counties in the US. Know that vandalism or graffiti that causes over $5,000 in damage is a felony in most states. We need to notify the police, take photographs, and cover or repair this damage as fast as possible, so as not to encourage more graffiti or vandalism.

While we never want to allow graffiti to overtake our walls and windows, it's important to know that painting over or removing gang or tagger-related signs, symbols, and messages could be potentially dangerous. Some graffiti is actually intended to be artistic by the operator of the spray paint cans. Other tagger-type graffiti is an attempt to be noticed and recognized within the tagger communities. Gang graffiti is used to mark neighborhood turf, set geographic gang boundaries, and to send messages and warnings to rival gangs and specific gang members.

Facility maintenance employees should work in pairs and watch for approaching people who may take issue with their work. Do not get into any verbal or physical confrontations with those suspected of doing the graffiti. Leave and call law enforcement, or return when it's safe to finish the job.

Action Steps:

Employee Responsibilities:

Report all graffiti that threatens specific people by name (employees, tenants, visitors, guests, etc.) to your supervisor.

Report all graffiti that threatens you by name to law enforcement and your supervisor.

If you feel unsafe at work as a result, you should discuss this with your supervisor.

Do not remove graffiti until a supervisor and/or law enforcement directs you to do so, and especially only after photographs are taken of the damage.

Supervisor Responsibilities:

Create a Security Incident Report of the damage for future reference.

Immediately contact your facility maintenance personnel to take photographs and remove any graffiti (only after a law enforcement report or if they have said they will not respond).

Notify law enforcement for any specifically threatening graffiti or significant damage caused to your facility or property.

If graffiti was directed at an employee, meet with him or her to discover the reasons why and to decide if that person should work from another location while law enforcement investigates.

Refer any targeted employees to your Employee Assistance Program for emotional support and managing their fears.

Reporting Procedures:

Work with law enforcement, if necessary.

WEATHER AND DISASTER PREPAREDNESS

Examples:

Earthquakes and subsequent building damage or evacuations. Weather events involving extreme heat or cold, storms, hurricanes, tornadoes, and shelter in place responses. Hazardous material spills or gas leaks in or near the building. Flooding from broken pipes, rain, rivers, or water sources.

Action Steps:

Pay attention to local disaster information and weather reports. Don't focus on rumors or gossip; use your common sense and get the facts from trained professionals. And just as importantly, when you hear it's time to evacuate, grab your personal items and go. You need to strike a balance between waiting to be told what do to and putting yourself in harm's way.

Some of the occupants of the World Trade Center Towers didn't survive on 9/11 because they waited to evacuate their floors until it was too late. If it's safer to shelter in place, do that. If you feel it's safer to leave, make a good decision and go, without always waiting to hear from local authorities if they are not on scene or in real-time communication with the media, your leadership team, or your facility.

Like during a real active shooter event, in a weather or disaster emergency, you should move away from your building and drive, run, or walk to alternative evacuation locations near your facility, like a church, store, mall, open government office, library, fire, police, or sheriff's station.

Employee Responsibilities:

As with many of the emergency situations discussed here, you need to take care of yourself and make sure you're safe and protected before you can help others. The lifeguards can't drown at the beach while making a rescue; they need to protect themselves first, then the person they're trying to save. You need to take care of yourself first, your co-workers second, and any visitors, vendors, customers, or taxpayers third. You are no good to anyone if you're not safe.

Don't rationalize someone else's irrational behavior, e.g., driving through an obvious flooded area, or staying inside a building during a gas leak because they don't believe it could harm them.

Supervisor Responsibilities:

Weather emergencies and other related disasters can affect the power supply for your facilities. If your facility has a generator and you have emergency response responsibilities, you'll need to know when and how it will operate, how much and what kind of fuel it uses (propane, diesel), how much power it can provide and for how long, and how often it's tested.

You need to have emergency response and evacuation systems, protocols, and policies already in place, long before a natural or man-made disaster happens. All this needs to be accompanied by regular drills. Doing the Run-Hide-Fight Active Shooter drill, a fire drill, an earthquake drill, or a weather-related drill once per year is usually sufficient. Those are usually scheduled drills, with plenty of notice given to the employees. But why not have an unscheduled drill about a simulated evacuation event to remind all employees to be vigilant and not just wait for the leadership team to tell them what's going to happen in advance?

Reporting Procedures:

Know who to tell, when to tell, and where and why to tell your designated safety and security stakeholders what is happening. Look and listen for emergency alerts that come to your e-mail system, cell phone texts, building-wide emergency PA announcements, or your Intranet or desk-level messaging systems. Follow the instructions of your federal, state, or local first-responders, local and national media, and local or federal disaster preparedness representatives.

APPENDIX

Some Additional Thoughts on the Safe and Secure Working Life

Don't just observe and report what you see, think and respond to what is happening to you or around you. Tell your safety and security stakeholders about issues they need to know about or safety or security equipment they need to install or fix.

Trust your instincts. Follow your intuition. If the little voice in your head says, "I wonder if I should call the police? Get my boss? Leave the area?" do any or all those things. Call 9-1-1 early rather than late.

Move away from dangerous people or dangerous situations. Don't ignore growing problems or people with escalating emotions. Make smart safety and security choices. Keep yourself safe first then help others. Get help from your co- workers or bosses early. You don't have to deal with difficult, challenging, or threatening people alone.

Use venting (let them talk or yell) and validation (use empathic phrases like, "I hear you" or "I'm not trying to make you mad" or "I can see you're upset") with angry people. Never say "Calm down!" to people who are not calm; it never works.

Use good "alignment" with angry or entitled people. We align best with others based on commonalities like age, race, gender, previous contacts, or past or shared experiences. Decide if you are the best person to handle their concerns or your co-workers or bosses are better choices.
Use active listening skills with people to show your concern: careful eye contact; nodding; building rapport; taking notes; using empathizing statements; asking questions; not interrupting; paraphrasing what they have said to you; seeking solutions they can agree with.

Don't trade security for convenience. Use your desk locks, file cabinet locks, door locks, vehicle locks, key cards, alarms, and passwords. Keep your facility keys, car keys, and key cards safe. Report any losses immediately.

Slow down and deepen your breathing in stressful or emergency situations. Take deep, controlled breaths to keep your mind and body oxygenated and stay out of the "fight or flight" mode.

Know when and where to Run, when and where to Hide, and when and how to Fight, in the rare event you're faced with an active shooter or mass attacker.

It's common to consider a good "shelter in place" safe room as having no windows, a lockable door, heavy barricade objects inside, and a way to shut off the lights. This could include a break room, restroom, training room, conference room, supervisor's office, storage room, file room, utility room, or a maintenance room. But your facility may have other non-traditional rooms which could meet a reasonable "safe room" definition, like a breastfeeding room, a meditation room, a nap room, or any safe space in the workplace where you can go with as many colleagues as you can to get out of the sight of an armed attacker.

Be a good, professional witness for the police and your employer. Some things that happen at work end up in litigation. Be ready to write down what happened after the situation is safe or stabilized.

The organization that is supposed to direct the safety of your organization or agency is known as OSHA – the Occupational Safety and Health Administration. All 50 states have a state-run office and the feds operate the national government office when it comes to keeping workplaces and employees safe from a variety of hazards ranging from falls to chemical exposures, and from bullets to machinery accidents. Companies of a certain size are supposed to complete and submit accident reports, known as "illness and injury reports," to their state OSHA offices within 8 hours of a fatality on the job and within 24 hours if an employee is seriously injured or hospitalized.

OSHA mandates all employers with something it calls the "General Duty Clause," which requires that "each employer furnish to each of its employees a workplace that is free from recognized hazards that are causing or likely to cause death or serious physical harm." All this means your employer has a legal obligation to keep you safe. But you have a duty as a vigilant employee to tell your bosses, co- workers, or facilities people if there are new or hidden hazards that they need to fix. You're just as much in charge of your safety as they are.

Speaking of acronyms, you may see various HR-related laws and policies for the Americans with Disabilities Act (ADA). This federal law was originally passed in 1990 and amended in 2008 to prevent workplace discrimination for job applicants or employees who have physical or psychological disabilities (visible or not). Employers must "reasonably accommodate" applicants or employees who ask for support in the ways they apply for or do their jobs. Note that you have to tell your employer, usually the HR department, (and provide a request letter from a physician) as to what accommodations they need to provide.

Retail and publicly-accessed businesses have the same legal requirement to provide safe and reasonable access to their facilities. We see this with handicapped parking spaces and ramps instead of stairs, restroom access, and lower counter heights. All businesses need to be aware of changing laws to support the disability community.

From a safety and security perspective, if you have any type of physical health or mental health limitations or restrictions that would make it difficult for you to evacuate your facility in an emergency, or shelter-in-place during a security event or an active shooter situation, or that keeps you from protecting yourself, you need to talk with both your medical doctor and your employer to see if you need an accommodation. There are lots of things employers can do and changes they can make to keep you safe, but they can only do so when you formally notify them. As just one example, the most common type of employee disability in the US is arthritis. If you have chronic joint pain, that can mean you have mobility issues as well. Don't wait to get help if you need it.

If your organization or agency distributes photo ID badges to all employees, make sure you participate in the process by always wearing yours. It's easy to get out of the habit, especially if your co-workers stop wearing theirs. We realize ID badges and the related access key cards that many people wear around their necks or keep clipped to their belts are not bulletproof shields in times of a real emergency, but they serve many useful purposes:

They help you identify who is an actual employee, or a vendor, or a visitor, or perhaps the family member of an employee or even an ex-employee who has come back for harmless or dangerous reasons.

They can help the police identify who is an employee and who might be a trespasser, intruder, or active shooter. The police will certainly have their hands full in a real active shooter event, but identifying the actual suspect is certainly high on their list.

Most employees who use access control key cards carry them in the plastic pocket in the lanyard around their neck along with their photo ID. These pockets can be useful for carrying other security-related items like a list of building public address system emergency code words.

You may also want to apply a stick-on label to the

back of your photo ID badge that has your emergency contact numbers, your blood type, and any medication allergies you have. This information can be useful for paramedics in a medical emergency.

Keep a fully charged flashlight at your desk or work station. It may be useful for you to keep a "Go Bag" at your desk, depending on the type of work you do, where your facility is located, and the weather conditions in your community. The "Go Bag" should contain what you need to be away from home for 24 hours.

Most companies that supply lockers to employees to store uniforms, tools, equipment, or personal property have (or need to have) a locker storage policy. If you regularly use a locker on company or agency property, it's important you know the policy language and you don't store anything that could get you fired or arrested.

Most policies usually say you cannot store "contraband," which is often defined as illegal drugs, prescription drugs not in a bottle with your name on it, firearms, ammunition, explosives, fireworks, obvious weapons (clubs, knives that aren't tools), stolen company or a co-worker's stolen property, and child pornography. Further, these policies usually specifically state you should know there is "no expectation of privacy" and your locker is subject to search at any time without a search warrant.

The policy language may say that the company can search your locker when they have "reasonable suspicion" that are conducted "for contraband only." In other words, they shouldn't remove your items randomly and toss them on a table for everyone to see. They should only remove things from your locker that are on the contraband list. These searches may be done by a responsible representative from HR, security, a manager, the company attorney, or the local police.

Speaking of weapons, almost everything in a workplace that is sharp, heavy, or dangerous can be used as a weapon. Most organizations have strict policies (usually found in their workplace violence prevention language) that prohibit loaded or even unloaded firearms inside their buildings. Some employees skirt this policy by keeping loaded or unloaded handguns, rifles, or shotguns in their personal vehicles while parked on company property. This may be illegal by state law and/or by company policy, so do your research before you bring any guns to work.

We've seen employees bring all manner of actual weapons to work, to show their co-workers or even to protect themselves from workplace violence. This includes: bear or wasp spray; shuriken throwing stars; nunchucks; billy clubs and nightsticks; sword canes; actual swords; and switchblades. If you don't legitimately use it to do your job, leave it at home.

In this age of terrorism awareness, your company may manufacture various products that have the potential to become hazardous materials used by international or domestic terrorists, working alone, as so-called "lone wolves" or in small groups or "cells." This could include chemicals, explosives, pesticides, fertilizers, radioactives, water, and even food and food by-products. If you work for a company where there is the possibility that your products could be stolen, manipulated, damaged, vandalized, or turned into some type of weapon, you need to be more than just a little vigilant as you go about your workday. Pay attention to what and who you see as you come and go each day. Tell your safety and security stakeholders what concerns you have about visitors, vendors, and strangers in or around your facility.

Many facilities will have internal and external storage areas that are fenced or caged off, to safely contain their most "theft-sensitive items." This could include expensive electronics devices (crates of desktops, laptops, or tablets); precious or recyclable metals; computer software; office supplies (toner, laser cartridges); hand and power tools; pallet jacks and forklifts; customer parts or merchandise to be shipped out; and manufacturing materials. If you work around these items and see these cages are regularly left unlocked (we often trade security for convenience), or you see unfamiliar people in and around these storage areas, tell your boss or the person who is in charge of that part of the facility. To say that things can get stolen "right under our noses" is often true because it doesn't always disappear in large chunks, but rather a little bit at a time.

If you work in a facility where cargo trucks come and go regularly, it's easy to take them for granted and not notice their movements. Like the cages and storage areas for theft-sensitive items, trucks can get stolen while parked up against loading docks, in the parking area of the yard, or even while waiting to be unloaded. Why? Because the drivers (again, trading security for convenience) often leave the keys in the ignitions. The average street thug or predatory homeless person may not know how to drive a semi-truck, but know that other trained crooks certainly do. They hijack construction equipment from job sites, semis from truck stops or warehouses, or steal from the loading areas while the real driver is on a bathroom break, getting coffee, or chatting with co-workers. If you see people you do not recognize around your truck fleets, tell one of your safety and security stakeholders about it.

You may be issued tools, equipment, uniforms, keys, electronic devices, and even a company or agency car or truck as part of your work. It's important to think of those things as "yours" and not just "the company's." You have a responsibility to safeguard those items as if you owned them. (Some companies may even charge you for items if they are lost, stolen, or damaged through your error.) Protect your equipment and work gear, especially if you have to take it into the field or on overnight trips.

Some employees think there is a never-ending supply of replacement tools or equipment, so they are careless in their handling of these items, wrongly believing that the company has a bottomless pit of money to replace them.

What they don't realize is that the more money the company saves, the easier it is for it to expand and hire more employees. Could it be possible that too many broken drill bits, personal protective equipment (PPE), crashed trucks, and lost tablets could add up to such an expense that the firm might not be able to hire someone or would have to let an employee go? You don't want to have to see them do that kind of math. Remind yourself and your co- workers that company assets, especially expensive ones, have a real monetary value. Protect what is given to you from theft, damage, or loss. The future of your job may depend upon it.

If you are tasked with holding on to financial, confidential, or proprietary company data; employee or HR-related information; client, customer, taxpayer, or vendor data, then always remember to lock your file cabinets even when you're at work. Just leaving your office for only a few moments provides just enough time for someone to come by and take a file folder or take one or more cell phone photos of the data inside it. It seems like overkill or an overreaction to do this, after all, real life isn't really like a spy movie, is it? Information gets stolen, leaked, manipulated, and sold every business day.

Similarly, use your office shredders daily, especially as you head out the door or go home. You may think your trash isn't important, but a clever social engineer/hacker knows otherwise. No company or agency information should be going into any trashcans. Do you think it's possible for someone who wants to get access to proprietary data could pay an outside janitorial service $50 a week to put all of the CEO's trash into an orange trash bag? (Easy to gather those out of the main dumpster at 2:00 a.m., which is why all outside trash dumpsters need to be kept padlocked until the moment the trash truck arrives.) When in doubt, if it doesn't need to be printed out and filed away, put it in the shredding bin.

Computer data gets stored in a variety of ways today. What started in the 80s and 90s as 5 1/4-inch floppy disks evolved to 3½-inch diskettes, went to zip disks, to portable hard drives, to CDs, then to laptops, tablets, smartphones, and now the Cloud. If you have any type of data on a computer-oriented physical device, you must keep it protected when you aren't using it. That means storing any computer software or related media in lockable file cabinets or desk drawers and password-protecting your computers, tablets, and phones.

You may be tempted to use your smartphone or a mini tape recorder to tape a bullying co-worker, angry boss, or entitled customer or client. Some of those taped rants can be useful to protect your reputation or to make a complaint to HR. Before you do that, check the laws in your state to see if you live in a one-party sufficient state or a two-party permission state. Some states allow taping without the other person's knowledge or consent. Most states require that the other person know you're doing it and also that he or she agrees to it. You'll notice that nearly every phone call you make to a business that uses a recorded message to screen your call will say, "All calls are recorded for quality control and training purposes." You can hang up if you don't want them to do that.

Keep all work-related travel plans confidential. Keep all travel-related information related to your bosses from skilled "social engineers," who may call or e-mail in seemingly harmless ways, like fake article writing, an "old friend" who really isn't, or calling to set up an in-person sales appointment for a product that doesn't exist. Don't give out where your boss is staying or when or where he or she is leaving and coming back. Just take a message.

Develop the habit of hard key protection, and report it immediately if any of your facility keys get lost or stolen and you cannot find them within two hours. Get over your embarrassment. Don't loan your keys to any employee who should not have access to them. He or she can make copies at lunch or over a long coffee break. It's easy to pay certain unethical locksmiths an extra $50 to make lots of copies of "Do Not Duplicate" keys.

People may visit you or your co-workers for a variety of reasons during the workday. This could include visitors who have a legitimate reason to be there, some who don't, and some who are in between. Pay attention to who comes and goes into your building and ask your boss or a co-worker to verify who is who.

Legitimate Visitors: Regular delivery vendors who have been approved, screened, or are escorted or supervised while on-site; invited clients, customers, or taxpayers, who have appointments or who are expected; repair people who are scheduled to do work while escorted; salespeople with a valid appointment; mail and package delivery people from the USPS, UPS, FedEx, Amazon, etc. All truck drivers, delivery people, or vendors who need to wait. i.e., to be paid, to pick up tools, or be assigned work, need to wait in a designated, secure area.

Not Legitimate Visitors: Vendors or salespeople who "pop in" without an appointment to try and sell a product or service without being asked or screened. (We've seen fire extinguisher salesmen come into a building uninvited, use "fire safety" as their ruse, "refill" all the dry fire extinguishers – that were not empty in the first place – and then send a big bill); angry customers, clients, or taxpayers who demand service; vendors who try to leave their products behind without permission (vending machines, copy machines, postage meters) and then try to claim later that the company "bought" their product.

Employees Who Have Been Fired: Or who have a civil restraining order against them, or who are on suspension should never be allowed on the property. This can include temporary employees, who either got fired, laid off, or did not have their employment contract renewed by the temp agency.

Visitors Who Need Further Screening: Family members (who may want to bring their pets), young children of employees, friends of employees, and former or retired employees will all need to follow established visitor sign-in and badging procedures. We don't need to be rude to these people, who may mean well, are friendly, and have no hidden agendas or motives to harm anyone, but it makes good business security sense to follow the visitor process.

None of the visitors in these categories should be allowed to wander around the facility without permission from your boss and/or the Human Resources, or Security Department. That includes no seemingly casual plant or facility tours, no taking of videos or photos, and no unescorted time for any of these visitors. We should identify the areas of your building that are absolutely off-limits to all non-employees, including the CEO's office, any labs or research and development working rooms, places where you have financial, customer, or employee data, any unreleased marketing materials, or product samples.

- All visitors must sign in at a reception area, get a badge (which they need to wear on a visible outer garment), and return it when they leave (or use the paper kind that expires by changing colors).

- The issue of sexual or racial harassment of our employees will always require management vigilance, current policies that support victims and punish perpetrators, and the necessary courage for all employees to report if they are harassed or witness other employees being harassed. (Just because it's not happening to you doesn't make it acceptable behavior. It's important for bystanders or direct witnesses to tell their supervisors, HR, or the company or agency attorney what they have seen, overheard, or were told by victim-employees, who may be too afraid of retaliation to report it themselves.)

- Consider how complex harassment situations can be with this scenario: A male employee on his lunch hour is sitting in the facility break room with another male co-worker, showing his colleague some porn videos on his personal cell phone. A third male employee walks through the break room, sees them laughing and joking about the images and keeps on going out the door. The two men did not show him the images or even speak to him at all. Later, the third employee complains to HR about what he witnessed.

• What do we think the first employee with the cell phone will say to defend his actions? "I was on my lunch break, not on company time. I was talking to my friend, who was not bothered by the videos. We were both laughing about them. I never asked the third employee to look at my phone. I never tried to show him what we were looking at. I never even spoke to that guy."

• Is this a reasonable defense? No, for the simple reason that although it may be true he did not show the other employee what they were looking at, his conduct is **unprofessional**, plain and simple. It doesn't matter if he was on his lunch break, he was still inside a company or agency facility, where the third employee has an expectation not to be exposed to pornography at work.

• All this means you have the right to a work environment that does not allow sexual or racial harassment from anyone, including directors, managers, or supervisors, co- workers or colleagues, and even vendors, visitors or customers. You need to tell your Human Resources representatives or safety and security stakeholders if these behaviors are happening to you or around you, so they can address it, investigate it, and stop it.

• Similar scenarios are possible that don't necessarily happen inside the actual workplace. You have the right not to be exposed to sexual or racial harassment during work-related activities or in settings that have a reasonable connection to the workplace. This includes driving to or flying to an offsite training program with a co-worker; sitting in an offsite hotel training room; or eating meals with colleagues in restaurants as part of work-related travel.

• You should not be expected to share a hotel room with a work colleague of the opposite sex. The presence of alcohol (in a hotel room or at a bar) is also not an excuse for bosses or co-workers to engage in sexually or racially- harassing behaviors, even if they are "just kidding" or "joking around with everybody." If you're subjected to jokes, comments, language, photos, videos, notes, or e- mails of a sexual or racial nature, or are physically touched in an unwanted way by anyone on a work-related business trip, you must report what happened (with as many details about dates, times, places, and offending conduct) to your Human Resources office.

• One way to gauge how safe and secure you are at your worksite is to take your own measurement of the work culture. What is the intuitive vibe you get when you consider your facility? Does it seem like security is ignored, minimized, or taken for granted that "nothing bad has ever happened here before"? Or do you see supportive evidence of vigilance, concern for the employees and the building? Do things feel loose or tight when it comes to access control and visitor policies? Do you see an investment in security devices, policies and procedures, new-employee orientation, occasional training programs, and the presence of guards?

• Does the leadership team seem connected and committed to employee security? Is the work culture casual (no real dress code, cubicles and work stations decorated, open and friendly communications between employees together or between bosses and employees)? Or is the work culture more formal (stricter dress code, work areas are kept to business-only posters and information, use of titles and Mr. or Ms. with senior leaders)? You can get a feel for the employee culture as soon as you walk into most businesses. What does your worksite feel like?

• One way to tell if your organization is fully prepared to deal with threats to the employees or the business is if your company or agency has a staffed, trained, and dedicated Threat Assessment Team (TAT).

These teams are often headed by the CEO or CEO's Office, managed by HR, and operated by HR and the Security Department, working together. These teams are usually trained by outside consultants who specialize in threat assessment and threat management. TATs should be staffed by the same safety and security stakeholders we discussed at the beginning of this book, with some departments needing to play multiple roles in smaller organizations:

- The CEO/CAO's and his or her representatives
- The General Manager or Plant Manager
- The City Manager or County Administrative Officer
- The Human Resources Director or Personnel Manager
- The Security Director or Manager
- Police or Sheriff's Department
- The IT Director or Manager
- Legal Counsel, County Counsel, or City Attorney
- The Facilities or Maintenance Director or Manager
- Risk Management
- Safety Office or Safety Officer
- Communications Director or Public Information Officer

When notified by company or agency leaders, concerned employees, or other safety and security stakeholders who may or may not be TAT members, the team will meet in person or by conference call to discuss a plan for:

- Threats or violence toward employees or our facilities.
- Threats or violence to any employee, by a current or former employee, visitor, vendor, or stranger.
- Employee-to-employee bullying, threats, or violence.
- High-risk employee discipline or terminations.
- Domestic violence crossovers from home to work involving employees.
- Threats to the facilities, including bomb threats.
- Cyber threats.
- Vexatious litigants, who sue for frivolous reasons.

Successful, functioning TATs are created, trained, staffed, and re-staffed as people change jobs or come on board the team.

- When thinking about the concept of a "Safe Room," for the rare possibility of an active shooter or active attacker, we can consider the best and not-as-best designs. The most effective safe room will have: a lockable door; be windowless or have shatter-proof glass; have one entry or exit door (or at least have sturdy locks on both, which the people inside can reach and lock quickly); a sturdy metal door frame; an accessible light switch that will keep the lights shut off (and not come back on due to motion in the room); it would be located off the main hallway (where the perpetrator is less likely to pass by or look for targets); there are barricade objects inside (desks, tables, moveable bookshelves, chairs, heavy furniture, equipment); there is a landline phone line installed; there are defensive protection items available (chairs, a fire extinguisher, heavy books, scissors); and, in a Perfect World: first-aid supplies, blankets, and water and snacks, in case the group has to lockdown for an extended period.

- A less suitable Safe Room would offer the opposite of these best must-haves from above: No door to lock down the room or a see-through glass door; an unlockable door (which too many offices have, in general); a half door – half window; too many entry/exit doors for the room, and they are not lockable; windows in the room with no blinds, shades, or curtains; nothing to hide behind; too much natural light; a room on the main traffic path (where the shooter is more likely to pass by, in search of his targets); and nothing inside the room to use in defense. In the imperfect world we live in when faced with the rare possibility of an armed attacker and an imperfect safe room, the best you may be able to do is turn the lights out, get on the floor, be quiet, and either wait for him to pass or attack him if he enters.

- Consider that you may be able to use your belt or the ID lanyard that holds your employee badge to secure a door. You can either wrap the belt or lanyard around the door closer mounted at the top of the doorframe or pull the doorknob toward the doorframe as you kneel down away from the door. Neither of these are ideal solutions, of course, but may be able to buy you enough time to save your life and the lives of the others hiding in the room with you. The goal, in the rare event of an encounter with an active shooter or armed attacker, is to deny or delay his entry enough to cause him to move on in search of other targets. These shooters already know that in most US cities, they only have about eight to ten minutes to do what they want to do before the police officers or sheriff's deputies arrive to engage with them. The cops know that these highly-stressful situations are not hostage negotiations, where the crook wants promises of money and a helicopter on the roof to escape. These are murder events, where the attacker will either shoot it out with the cops, kill himself, or wait for the cops to have to shoot him in a "suicide by cop" situation.

- A hard but reasonable question that comes up a lot in our workplace violence prevention training programs is whether or not to unlock the door of a safe room to allow one or more employees to come inside. The scenario is certainly possible: several employees hear shots fired and because they can't get out of the building safely, they run to a break room, restroom, training room, storage room, file room, or other room that they can lock and secure. They barricade the door with heavy furniture, move away from the doorway (known by the police as the "Fatal Funnel" because the shooter may fire through the doorway in the hopes he can kill people he cannot see), spread out inside, quietly call 9-1-1 if it's safe to do so, and wait for the arrival of the police.

Suddenly, they hear a vigorous pounding on the door, as one or more of their terrified co-workers wants to come inside. It's a horrible dilemma and an awful choice to have to make: do we open the door to try and save our colleagues but risk the attacker gaining entry and shooting us? Or do we stay quiet and not alert the attacker to our position and hope that our colleagues can find a safe room of their own? A real active shooter situation is a frightening, stressful, life-changing event, even without having to choose between saving your colleagues inside the room or saving your colleagues outside the room.

No one wants to make that choice, so we advise you to take the risk, open the door quickly, and pull them inside to safety.

Throughout this book, we have always advised that the best response to the rare possibility of an active shooter in your facility is not just Run, or Hide, or Fight, but doing all three, in separate locations or all together in one place, out of order, as necessary. As the situation changes and your survival instincts kick in, protect yourself and others the best way you can.

You may need to Fight back as soon as you come around the corner of your office hallway and tackle the shooter as he is walking away from you in search of his targets. You may need to Hide first, then Run to a safer location, as soon as the attacker leaves your building and goes to another across the parking lot. Much of what you do and where you go will depend on the attacker's plan and behavior and the arrival of the police.

If we look at the attacker's behaviors by reviewing the hundreds of active shooter events that have happened in this country and overseas, we can make some conclusions (that are not carved in stone and may change as these attackers become more tactical and sophisticated in their methods).

Overall, we have not seen many shooters shoot through wooden or metal doors to kill people hiding in the room. (They have tended to shoot through glass entry/exit doors in office lobbies or school foyers, which is why we have talked so often about the value of hiding behind bullet-stopping Cover versus hiding behind things that only provide Concealment.) We have heard of no incidents where the shooter has attempted to gain entry to a safe room where employees are hiding by impersonating the police. This is not to say either of these two behaviors will never occur, only that they are unlikely.

The 19-year-old school shooter in the February 2018

mass attack at the Marjory Stoneman Douglas High School in Parkland, FL is said to have pulled one of the fire alarms on campus, near the end of the school day. His goal, we assume, was to move people out of the relative safety of their classrooms and into the hallways and other evacuation points, where he could shoot them. This is a rare behavior among mass attackers.

One of the earliest examples happened in June 1991, involving shooter Larry Hansel, a former employee of Elgar Corporation in San Diego, CA, who returned to the facility and killed two senior executives. Hansel pulled the fire alarm in the building and this caused the employees to evacuate into his path. (Steve Albrecht interviewed Hansel in prison in 2020.)

There are two sides to the fire alarm issue: while most active shooters have not pulled a fire alarm to start a mass evacuation and make it easier to shoot people, for that same reason, we should not ever pull the fire alarm during a mass shooting event to "help evacuate people."

Pulling a building fire alarm, both when there is not a real fire and during an active shooter situation is a bad idea, so don't do it.

Modern building techniques, state fire codes, and advanced fire detection, alarm, and suppression equipment make building fires in offices and factories quite rare. That's not to say they can't happen but that it's highly unlikely they will. But as we noted in the section of this book on fire emergencies, we need to be trained to respond correctly in a real fire emergency. This includes annual fire drills, the use of floor wardens for multi-story buildings, and regular inspections by the local Fire Marshal.

As such, we need to treat a building fire alarm for what it is for: the presence of a building fire, not an active shooter event.

ABOUT THE AUTHOR

Dr. Steve Albrecht, SHRM PHR, ASIS CPP, ATAP CTM
As a trainer, speaker, author, and consultant, Dr. Steve Albrecht is internationally known for his expertise in high-risk HR issues and security concerns. He provides consulting, threat assessments, site security surveys, corrective coaching, webinars, and training seminars in workplace and school violence prevention, library security, harassment prevention, substance abuse awareness, team building, conflict resolution, customer service, and stress management.

In 1994, Dr. Albrecht co-wrote **Ticking Bombs: Defusing Violence in the Workplace,** one of the first business books on workplace violence. He has interviewed three workplace murderers in prison. Besides his work as a conference presenter and keynote speaker, he appears in the media and on the Internet, as a source on workplace violence, school violence, library security, crime, and terrorism.

Dr. Albrecht holds a doctoral degree in Business Administration (D.B.A.), an M.A. in Security Management, a B.A. in English, and a B.S. in Psychology. He has been a trainer for 36 years and is board certified in human resources, security management, employee coaching, and threat management. He holds these designations: SHRM Certified Professional; ASIS Certified Protection Professional; and ATAP Certified Threat Manager.

He has written 26 books on leadership, criminal justice, security, library security, and crisis management.

Steve retired from the San Diego Police Department, where he had worked for almost 16 years, both as a full-time officer and later as a reserve sergeant. He spent six years in the Domestic Violence Unit, where he handled over 1,500 cases.

He is a former National Board member and two-term president of the San Diego chapter of the Association of Threat Assessment Professionals (ATAP).

ABOUT THE AUTHOR

Robert C. May, J.D., WCCA, CPFI
Dr. Robert May is the former Risk Management Program Manager for the California Joint Powers Insurance Authority. His responsibilities included providing risk management guidance to over 100 Authority members as well as to five regional risk managers for the Authority.

His areas of expertise include contracts or agreements for administration for appropriate risk transfer and insurance specification language; providing input on risk exposures associated with city or county-sponsored activities and events; providing legal support and field assistance; and discussing program coverage issues with agencies. Bob also conducts leadership training for city council and elected or appointed board members. Bob provides guidance in litigation employment matters including reviewing internal investigation reports.

Bob's main career focus has been in the public sector. Prior to joining the California JPIA in 2007, he worked for over thirty years in the California fire service. He is a Level 1 and 2 instructor of the California State Fire Training System. Bob has received certification in Workers Compensation Claims Administration from the Insurance Institute. Bob is also a certified Emergency Medical Technician.

Bob is nationally known for his expertise in the field of risk management. He has a broad depth of municipal and special district experience and has conducted training in organizational behavior, labor relations, strategic planning, and career development. Bob teaches leadership training for city councils and special district boards to help in their understanding of council/manager form of governance. Bob has written several white papers on dealing with the homeless and Hepatitis A. He regularly presents on workplace violence, crisis management, media relations, and safety in the workplace.

Bob holds a B.S. degree in law, a J.D. degree, and two California teaching credentials. He is a licensed private investigator in the state of California.

ORDERING INFORMATION

To order more copies of this book, please contact:

www.MainstreamUnlimited.com/order

For large print runs, we can customize this book with your organization's name on the cover and include a message from the senior member of your leadership team.

A Note About Future Editions of This Book:

We've tried to consider every possible safety and security event you're likely to encounter as an employee or as a supervisor. If there are items we need to add or issues we need to cover in future editions of this book, please send us an email at Book@mainstreamunlimited.com

www.ingramcontent.com/pod-product-compliance
Lightning Source LLC
Chambersburg PA
CBHW060030210326
41520CB00009B/1074